BOOK ENDORSEMENT

*** A good reference guide on issues related not only to the sustainability of projects and programs but also to the sustainability of systems, institutions and organizations

    – **Dr. Mrs. Mercy M. Tembon, Country Manager, the World Bank, Burundi**

*** An excellent textbook addressing contemporary project management concepts, principles and techniques affecting the implementation of projects in various sectors of the economy

    – **Dr. William Dadson, Lincoln University of Pennsylvania, Oxford, PA, USA**

D0433392

PROJECT SUSTAINABILITY

PROJECT
SUSTAINABILITY

A Comprehensive Guide to Sustaining Projects, Systems and Organizations in a Competitive Marketplace

JOHN N. MORFAW, MBA

iUniverse, Inc.
Bloomington

Project Sustainability
A Comprehensive Guide to Sustaining Projects, Systems and Organizations in a Competitive Marketplace

iUniverse books may be ordered through booksellers or by contacting:

iUniverse
1663 Liberty Drive
Bloomington, IN 47403
www.iuniverse.com
1-800-Authors (1-800-288-4677)

ISBN: 978-1-4620-1271-8 (sc)
ISBN: 978-1-4620-1272-5 (e)

Printed in the United States of America

iUniverse rev. date: 08/08/2011

A DEDICATION

This book is dedicated to my dear wife, Pamela Asangong Morfaw (Lady Pammy MOR) for her sacrifices and support towards my personal and professional goals. It is also dedicated to lovely children-Nkengafac Esthel Morfaw and Muyang Miriam Morfaw, best known as "The Mor Sisters".

CHARTS AND TABLES

CHART 3:01- GENERAL PROCESS PROCEDURE. 32
CHART 3:02- PROCESS FLOW CHART SYMBOLS 33
CHART 3:02:01- AFFINITY DIAGRAM 34
CHART 3:02:03- MATRIX DIAGRAM 35
CHART 3:02:04- GANTT CHART 36
CHART 3:02:07- CAUSE AND EFFECT DIAGRAM 37
CHART 3:03:02- PARETO CHART. 38
CHART 3:03:03-BAR CHART 39
CHART 3:03:04- RUN CHART 39
CHART 3:03:05- PIE CHART 40
CHART 3:03:06- HISTOGRAM. 40
CHART 3:03:07- SCATTER DIAGRAM 41
CHART 4:01- QUALITY ORGANIZATIONAL STRUCTURE 42
CHART 4:02- TRADITIONAL ORGANIZATIONAL STRUCUTRE . . . 48

TABLE 1:02:08- SOME CAUSES OF PROJECT FAILURES. 18
TABLE 1:02:09- PROJECTS, PROGRAMS AND PORTFOLIO
                MANAGEMENT COMPARED 20
TABLE 3:03:01- DATA SHEET. 38
TABLE 4:03:03- TRADITIONAL MANAGEMENT AND TQM
                COMPARED 50
TABLE 7:09:02- CHARACTERISTICS OF M & E 108
TABLE 7:09:05- DIFFERENCE BETWEEN M & E 112

ACRONYMS

- ❖ **CQI-** Continuous Quality Improvement
- ❖ **ISO-** International Organization for Standardization
- ❖ **NGO-** Non-Governmental Organization
- ❖ **QC-** Quality Control
- ❖ **QA-** Quality Assurance
- ❖ **CPM-** Critical Path method
- ❖ **M & E-** Monitoring and Evaluation
- ❖ **TQC-** Total Quality Control
- ❖ **TQM-**Total Quality Management
- ❖ **ANSI-** American National Standards Institute
- ❖ **SAP-** Structural Adjustment Program
- ❖ **S.M.A.R.T-** Specific, Measurable, Attainable, Timely
- ❖ **S.W.O.T** – Strength, Weaknesses, Opportunities, Threats
- ❖ **HRM-** Human Resources Management
- ❖ **ICT-** Information and Communication Technology
- ❖ **M.B.O-** Management By Objectives
- ❖ **PERT-** Program Evaluation and Review technique
- ❖ **PSM-** Project Sustainability Management
- ❖ **PMO-** Project Management Organization
- ❖ **SMO-** Sustainable Management Organization
- ❖ **SIP-** Strategic Implementation Plan

Acknowledgement

Heartfelt thanks goes to R. Max Wideman of Vancouver, British Columbia, Canada for permitting me to exploit and use his Dictionary of Project Management Terms*. Max Wideman has also motivated and encouraged me to follow the authorship career path and has also profiled me in his personal website for project management professionals.

Special gratitude goes to Ms. Lauri "Lee" Elliott, President/CEO of the Washington DC-based consulting firm-Conceptualee Inc. for her analytical review of the manuscript and her very constructive suggestions. Special thanks also goes to Mr. Shelvin D. Longmire, Chair of the Global Entrepreneurship and Enterprise Management Center at Morgan State University, Baltimore, Maryland and Dr. Lebong N. Morfaw, an independent consultant in Lanham, Maryland, for their advice and continuous insistence on the authoring of a top-notch book.

I am deeply indebted to Mr. Eric Chinje, Manager at the World Bank Institute in Washington DC and Dr. Mrs. Mercy M. Tembon, World Bank Country Manager in Burundi, and Dr. Dominic Ntube of the World Bank Group Africa Diaspora Program for their down-to-earth support, referrals and suggestions for a more qualitative product with a wide reaching impact. I am very thankful to Dr. Valentine James, Provost and Academic Vice-President and Chair of the Sustainability Institute of Clarion University of Pennsylvania for inviting me to join the Advisory Board of this prestigious institute in order to promote sustainable development around the World.

Professor Januarius J. Asongu of Rockford College, Illinois, USA and Chairman/CEO of the Institute for Research in Global Business (IRGB) and the Chartered Financial Assistance have shared a lot of ideas and knowledge about the initiation, conceptualization, design and implementation of projects and the sustainability of businesses in the marketplace. Great appreciation also goes to Dr. William K. Dadson of the Department of Business and Information Technology of Lincoln University of Pennsylvania and His Royal Highness Chief Alex Taku for their motivation and encouragement towards the realization of this book project.

Great appreciation goes to Mr. Michael Nkeng, CEO of Chariot Hotel Corporation, Cameroon West Africa and Chariot Giving Inc. Bowie, Maryland, USA, Mr. Joseph F. Mubang, President/CEO of First Choice Health Services Inc., Mr. Benedict A. Foretia, CEO of Lifecare Inc., all in Washington DC, and Mr. Nicodemus Morfaw, CEO of Morfaw's Tax Solutions in Bowie, Maryland, USA for their generosity and especially their financial support towards the publication of the book. The marketing and promotional inputs from Mr. Ivo Tasong, President and COO of AttivaSoft Company, and Mr. Jude and Marceline Nyambi of The Hampton Conference Center in Maryland are greatly appreciated.

My dear wife Mrs. Pamela Asangong-Morfaw (Lady Pammy MOR) has been very instrumental in this project and her ideas, encouragement, love, affection, protection and moral support have been great catalysts towards its realization.

*Terms abstracted from the *Wideman Comparative Glossary of Project Management Terms* are © R. Max Wideman: http://www.maxwideman.com, 2005 and reproduced with permission. For the original source of individual terms, please refer to:
http://www.maxwideman.com/pmglossary/PMGloss_Sources.htm.

FOREWORD

This book, "Project Sustainability", explores some of the most exciting frontiers of modern management and especially project planning and management and sustainability in the marketplace. Business consultants, students, government and non-governmental organizations and leadership and management organizations will find a body of enjoyable and useful information within the covers of this book. The chapters expound on learned knowledge of contemporary business environment and through the pages one will discover how profound the influence of sustainability is not only in our daily lives but also for social, economic, cultural, educational and political institutions.

The inspiration for this book arose from the desire to enlighten and instill a greater appreciation in the business community and society as a whole about this very challenging subject-project sustainability and to inspire business owners, stakeholders, researchers, consultants and students to explore its fascination application. This discipline is both challenging and rewarding and demands the best of human intellect, integrity, character, experience, originality, imagination, dexterity, networking and effective and efficient communication. This book represents an enthusiastic approach to the management of projects and business undertakings. It is a unique tribute to many business theories on efficiency and effectiveness of the management of human, material and financial resources for maximum productivity and sustainability.

The author, Mr. John Morfaw is highly experience and has elaborated on his views and opinions on how contemporary business is facing a lot of challenges on sustainability in the marketplace due to the influence of technology, political changes, cultural transformation of the society and the workplace, the alteration of the environment and the changing pattern of the production of goods and services.

Dr. Mrs. Mercy M. Tembon
World Bank Country Manager
Bujumbura, Burundi
April, 2011

PREFACE

The concept of "Sustainable Development" was first advocated by the Brundtland Report mandated by the United Nations in 1983 through the World Commission on Environment and Development to propose solutions to the world's problems on environment and development. This commission led by Gro Harlem Brundtland sought to define the form of development which could solve the problems of poverty without increasing the problems cause by affluence. The Commission defined Sustainable Development as "development which meets the present without compromising the ability of future generations to meet their own needs". The commission proposed policy changes in population and human resources, food security, species and ecosystem conservation, energy, industry and urban settlements. The "Sustainable Development" concept is sweeping across the entire world involving almost all social, economic, cultural, educational and political institutions. It is now unrealistic to think of running a program or project without a concrete plan for its long-term viability and ultimate sustainability in the very competitive marketplace. The current economic and financial crisis plaguing world economies has been a "litmus test" on their sustainability and long-term viability of many banks and other financial institutions as well as political, educational and economic organizations.

Generally, the major components of "Sustainable Development Projects" are Ecology or Environment, Economics, politics and Social Welfare. The projects should be viable, expedient, acceptable and adaptable to citizens and the environment and range from roads to bridges, buildings, education, social projects, business undertakings and other projects altering environmental landscapes. According to Martinuzzi et al, (2009), holistic approach, long-term orientation, large spatial and institutional scale, risk and uncertainty, values and ethical considerations, participation, capacity building should always be incorporated and integrated in the objects. The authors further state that the definition of "Sustainable Development Projects" should be project considerations such as project objectives, work break-down structures, project deadlines, project resources, revenues, costs, project organizational culture and the project management process.

It is a truism that Project Sustainability remains a major challenge nowadays not only to developing countries but to developed countries as well due to technological transformation, political changes, corruption, nepotism, deregulation, financial instability characterized by insolvency and liquidity problems, and other social, cultural, environmental and economic factors. A great variety of projects continued to be implemented at a huge cost often above budget and time and this often affect their sustainability. World famous sustainable business projects such as Ford Motors, Mercedes Benz, Sony Corporation, Toyota, Honda, Sharp, Microsoft, Wal-Mart, Home Depot etc have been able to sustain themselves in the marketplace they have been scalable, manageable, extensible, expandable and their products and services adapted to customers and the changing environment.

A great concept which has emerged to address the issues related to the effective and efficient implementation of sustainable projects and related activities is Project Sustainability Management (PSM). This involves the strategic management of structures, systems, activities, rules and regulations, resources, benchmarks and parameters all put in place to determine the sustainability of projects. This book references the "Bill of Rights for the Planet" or the "Hannover Principles", developed by William McDonough Architects which elaborate on design principles necessary for sustainability.

This book focuses on how effective and efficient feasibility studies, conceptualization, design, monitoring and evaluation of projects can help to enhance their sustainability in the marketplace. It also evaluates the contribution of other concepts such as Six Sigma Methodology, Configuration Management, Capacity Building, Knowledge Management, Project Planning and Management, human resources management and their impact project implementation and its sustainability. This book also elaborates on basic quality improvement tools such as SWOT Analysis, process flow analysis, cost-benefit and cost-effectiveness analysis, quality organizational structures, systems analysis, feasibility studies, change management, issue management, risk management process and organizational behavior and team building which help to analyze and evaluate various quality management processes.

The modus operandi of this book is to analyze and evaluate the effects and impact of various project implementation models on the sustainability of projects. A concise and comprehensive Sustainability Plan is fully developed for this purpose. Fundamental quality management concepts such as Quality Assurance (QA), Quality Control (QC) and Continuous Quality Improvement (CQI) have been fully explained in the book. Total Quality Management tools such as Affinity Diagrams, Tree Diagrams, Matrix Diagrams, Gantt Charts, Relationship Diagrams, and Cause and Effects Diagrams, and various TQM statistical tools such as Data Sheets, Pareto Charts, Bar Charts, Run Charts, Pie Charts, Histograms and Control Charts used in project analysis and evaluation are fully discussed in the book. Some of the major causes of the failures of projects are also outlined.

The book is split into eight well-defined chapters: Project Management and Project Sustainability defined, Strategic Management Organization (SMO), Culture, Principles and Characteristics, Process Development and Management, Sustainable Management Organizational Structure, the Sustainable Implementation Plan (SIP), templates for various Project Management Processes and Project Sustainability Management (PSM). Further, the book includes an exhaustive glossary of significant terms, strategic implementation training forms, common business jargons and common business acronyms.

The book is intended as a consulting manual for scholars, researchers, professional consultants in project management, quality assurance, quality improvement and general management, health research institutions, hospitals and clinics, health insurance companies, small and large-scale businesses, Governmental and Non-Governmental and other international organizations involved in the implementation of projects around the world. This book is also intended to be a textbook for undergraduate and graduate students in business schools, vocational and other trade centers.

Washington, DC, USA   John N. Morfaw, MBA, PM
May, 2011.

Website: www.tanyimorproject.com
Email: sirjohnmor@yahoo.com

TABLE OF CONTENTS

CHAPTER ONE

1:00- Introduction. 1
1:01- Project Sustainability 3
1:02- Project Management 9

CHAPTER TWO

2:00- Project Sustainability Management (PSM). 22
2:01- Project Sustainability Management Plan 23
2:02- Some Sustainability Society Indexes 25
2:03- Project Sustainability Management Checklist. 26

CHAPTER THREE

3:00- Sustainable Process Development 29
3:01- Process Flow Chart. 31
3:02- Total Quality Management Tools 34
3:03- Total Quality Management Statistical Tools 37

CHAPTER FOUR

4:00- Sustainable Organizational Structure 42
4:01- Structure 43
4:02- Team Roles and Responsibilities. 45
4:03- Traditional Management and Integrated Management
(TQM) Compared. 47

CHAPTER FIVE

5:00- Strategic Implementation Plan (SIP) 51
5:01- Top Management Commitment. 53
5:02- Development of Corporate Strategic Plan 54
5:03- Development of an Organizational Structure 59
5:04- Development of Implementation Budget 61
5:05- Quality Council, Teams and Panels 61

5:06- Starting an Awareness Program 61
5:07- Training of Team Leaders and Facilitators. 62
5:08- Conduction of an Initial Status Survey. 62
5:09- Documented Implementation Plan 63
5:10- Quality System Documentation. 63
5:11- Document Control 64
5:12- Implementation 64
5:13- Internal Quality Audit 65
5:14- Management Review 65
5:15- Pre-Assessment Audit. 65
5:16- Certification and Registration 66
5:17- Continuous Quality Improvement (CQI) 66
5:18- Some Benefits of Strategic Implementation 68

CHAPTER SIX

6:01- Total Quality Management Fundamentals 70
6:02- Total Quality Management and The Paradigm Shift. 74
6:03- Principles of Total Quality Management 74
6:04- Basic Total Quality Management Framework. 79
6:05- Basic Tenets of Total Quality Management. 80
6:06- The Gurus of Total Quality Management. 81
6:07- Total Quality M Management Culture. 85
6:08- Total Quality Management as a Foundation. 87
6:09- Ten Steps to Total Quality Management 88
6:10- History of Quality Paradigms. 88
6:11- Total Quality Leadership 89

CHAPTER SEVEN

7:00- Other Sustainable Management Concepts 91
7:01- Six Sigma Methodology. 91
7:03- TQM and the International Organization for Standardization
        (ISO) Series Standards. 94
7:04- Configuration Management. 96
7:05- Human Resource Management 97
7:06- Capacity Building 99

7:07- Knowledge Management 100
7:08- Swot Analysis 102
7:09- Monitoring and Evaluation 106

CHAPTER EIGHT

8:00- Sustainable Project Management Processes 114
8:01- The Project Plan Process 115
8:02- Feasibility Study Process 119
8:03- Quality Plan Process 120
8:04- Change Manageent Process 121
8:05- Risk Management Process 122
8:06- The Business Plan 123
8:07- The Marketing Plan 125
8:08- The Project Proposal Template 126

CONCLUSION 137

−   **APPENDIX:** 139
    −   Glossary 139
    −   Strategic Implementation Training Forms 150
            1) Daily Organizer 150
            2) Weekly Organizer 151
            3) Monthly Organizer 152
            4) Customer Contact Sheet 153
            5) Goals/Objectives Sheet 154
            6) Quality Improvement Structure: 155
            7) Process Improvement Teams: 156
            8) Roles And Responsibilities: 157
            9) Developing Meeting Ground Rules: 158
            10) Meeting Ground Rules: 160
            11) Drafting A Team Charter 161
            12) Team Charter: 162
            13) Meeting Agenda: 163
            14) Minutes Record 164
            15) Attendance Log: 165

16) Team Project Record 166
19) Employee Satisfaction Survey 167
20)-Problem-Solving Techniques 168
21) Components of Structure, Process and Output 169
‒   Common Business Jargons 170
‒   Common Business Acronyms 177

‒   **BIBLIOGRAPHY** 181

‒   **INDEX** 185

‒   **ABOUT THE AUTHOR** 193

ORGANIZATION OF THE BOOK

This book comprises eight chapters with an appendix as follows:

Chapter one deals with the definitions and characteristics of Project Sustainability and project Management, dimensions, measurement and the metrics.

Chapter Two examines the Project Sustainability Management (PSM) which is a new concept dealing with the strategies to effectively and efficiently manages any sustainability plan.

Chapter Three looks at the impact of process development and flowcharting on design and the effects of TQM management and statistical tools on project analysis and evaluation.

Chapter Four tackles the organizational structure of a quality management organization, compares and contrasts traditional and integrated (TQM) management approaches, defines the roles and responsibilities of the Quality Council, teams and panels on an organization.

Chapter Five examines a classic Sustainable Project Implementation Plan and its related processes such as top level commitment, corporate strategic plan, budget, awareness programs, training, survey, auditing, and management review and outlines the benefits of the implementation of a Sustainable Project Management Program in an organization.

Chapter Six tackles the TQM framework, discusses the basic tenets of TQM, provides an insight on the Gurus of TQM such as Edward Deming and his 14 point for quality improvement, Joseph Juran and his 14 steps to quality improvement, Philip Crosby and his 14 steps to quality improvement, Walter Shewhart, Kaoru Ishikawa and Shigeo Shingo. The chapter finally outlines some major causes of project failures.

Chapter Seven makes and insight on other management concepts impacting Project Sustainability model such as the Six Sigma methodology, the International Organization for Standardization (ISO), Configuration Management, Human Resource Management, Capacity Building, SWOT Analysis and the S.M.A.R.T techniques and Monitoring and Evaluation.

Chapter Eight elaborates on various templates of project management processes such as project planning, feasibility studies, quality planning, change management process, risk management process, the business plan, the marketing plan and the project proposal

The Appendix comprise a glossary, some common business jargons, a comprehensive list of Sustainability Management training forms, some common business acronyms, bibliography and an index.

CHAPTER ONE

1:00- INTRODUCTION

Project Sustainability is now a common syndrome related to the management of projects, programs, institutions, organizations, people and other entities requiring effective and efficient production, marketing, distribution and the delivery products and services. Generally, for projects to be sustained certain metrics and standards need to be set from project identification through feasibility studies, formulation, design, appraisal, funding, implementation, monitoring and evaluation. It is a proven truism that most projects are failing because of the lack of an appropriate sustainability plan. It is therefore very necessary for a comprehensive analysis of the social, economic, legal, cultural, educational and political environments for project implementation. The project philosophy, mission, vision, values, goals and objectives should be fully articulated and stated in the plan. The involvement of stakeholders and advocates is of paramount importance since it facilitates some logistical preparation. Beneficiary assessment, legal and regulatory framework studies, marketing and competition analysis, partnership development and institutional analysis give room for effective and efficient implementation

Project Management and Total Quality Management (TQM) complement each other when it comes to implement because one is a concept and the other is a process. This creates a very strong and symbiotic relationship between them. They are all achieved through employee empowerment in decision making, the use of facilitated teams in the organization, individual responsibility for products and services and a strong customer service orientation, working from a set of values envisioning a mission, maintaining commitment, sustaining motivation, prioritizing tasks, cooperating with others, communicating effectively and seeking to continuously learn and grow.

Project sustainability analysis will determine project relevance, acceptability, political expediency, viability and adaptability of the project. Other factors such as financial analysis, risk analysis, communication and network determination, operational plan, training, human resource development and capacity building, environmental and community analysis all help to determine the sustainability of projects. Funding requirement have to be analyzed and evaluated to determine whether the project is a franchise, independent project, cooperative, joint venture, Non-Governmental or Governmental organization etc.

A project always describes the rationale, demand and supply basis, costs, anticipated outcomes or outputs and performance metrics which all need to be met for it to quality for funding. Demographic studies analyses needs, income, interests, cultures, education and other human, social and economic factors in order to determine affordability. The legal and regulatory framework deals with licenses and authorizations and various rules, regulations, by-laws and protocols required by law for the Implementation of projects in that environment. Technically, the Information, Communication and Technology (ICT) infrastructure required for the project should be properly assessed especially access to modern technology and systems.

Financial sustainability of a project depends on effective and efficient budgeting. Expenses and costs, projections, revenues, depreciations, profit and lost statements have to be fully factored in. The financial Bottom Line analysis of the project is key and should prove profitability calculations or any variations explained and justified.

The S.M.A.R.T technique (Specific, Measurable, Attainable, and Realistic, Timely) has become a main model for business project implementation because it sets some baseline for evaluation. The S.W.O.T Analysis (Strengths, Weaknesses, Opportunities, and Threats) has facilitated the identification of both problems and potentials for the projects in order to determine their sustainability as well.

Project Sustainability Management (PSM) is now gaining grounds in project management and is changing the dynamics of the implementation of a variety of projects.

1:01- PROJECT SUSTAINABILITY

Sustainability is a systematic concept relating to the continuity of economic, social, institutional and environmental aspects of human society as well as the non-human environment. It is characteristic of a process or state that a business can be maintained at a certain level indefinitely. The Brundtland Commission of the United Nations in 1987 defined sustainable development as "development that meets the needs of the present without compromising the ability of future generations to meet their own needs". But the definition of sustainability may vary depending on the area of studies or interaction or the context or situations over many scales of space and time from small ones to global balance of production and consumption.

The philosophical and analytical framework of sustainability draws on and connects with many different disciplines and fields and has tended to be problem-driven and oriented towards guiding decision-making. The focus ranges from the total carrying capacity (sustainability) of planet Earth to the sustainability of economic and social sectors, ecosystems, countries, municipalities, neighborhoods, home gardens, individual lives, individual goods and services, occupations, lifestyles, behavior patterns, academic and research institutions, political institutions and business operations.

Business sustainability is a state where the demands placed upon the environment by people and commerce can be met without reducing the capacity of the environment to provide for future generations. The fundamental principle is for businesses to perform tasks and services that are effectively and efficiently produced and promote sustainability in the society as a whole. In order for a business to be sustainable in the marketplace services and products should have little or no competition in terms of image, power, quality, packaging, prices etc? Instead products and services should be provided in a way so as reduce consumption, energy use, distribution costs, economic concentration and other forms of business and environmental damage.

Generally, the main strategies for managing an organization according to sustainable development principles are stakeholder analysis, development of policies and objectives, designing and executing and implementation plan, developing a supportive corporate culture, developing measures and standards of performance, preparing periodic reports and enhancing internal monitoring processes.

The concept of sustainability has been widely embraced in the environmental arena and in the construction industry. This has been exemplified by the "Bill of Rights of the Planet" or the "Hannover Principles" developed by William McDonough Architects for the EXPO 2000 held in Hannover, Germany.

The "Bill of Rights for the Planet" stipulates the following:

1. Insist on the right of humanity and nature to co-exist in a healthy, supportive, diverse, and sustainable condition.
2. Recognize Interdependence. The elements of human design interact with and depend on the natural world, with broad and diverse implications at every scale. Expand design considerations to recognizing even distant effects.
3. Respect relationships between spirit and matter. Consider all aspects of human settlement including community, dwelling, industry, and trade in terms of existing and evolving connections between spiritual and material consciousness.
4. Accept responsibility for the consequences of design decisions upon human well-being, the viability of natural systems, and their right to co-exist.
5. Create safe objects of long-term value. Do not burden future generations with requirements for maintenance or vigilant administration of potential danger due to the careless creations of products, processes, or standards.

6. Eliminate the concept of waste. Evaluate and optimize the full life-cycle of products and processes, to approach the state of natural systems in which there is no waste.

7. Rely on natural energy flows. Human designs should, like the living world, derive their creative forces from perpetual solar income. Incorporate this energy efficiently and safely for responsible use.

8. Understand the limitations of design. No human creation lasts forever and design does not solve all problems. Those who create and plan should practice humility in the face of nature. Treat nature as a model and mentor, not an inconvenience to be evaded or controlled.

9. Seek constant improvement by the sharing of knowledge. Encourage direct and open communication between colleagues, patrons, manufacturers and users to link long term sustainable considerations with ethical responsibility, and re-establish the integral relationship between natural processes and human activity.

This Bill of Rights for the Planet was adopted by the World Congress of the International Union of Architects in June 1993.

Some dimensions of project sustainability are:-

1- Institutional Stability
2- Continued operation and maintenance of project facilities
3- Continuous flow of net benefits
4- Maintenance of environmental stability
5- Equitable sharing and distribution of project benefits
6- Continued community participation

1:01:01- Some Examples and Principles of Project Sustainability

1- Replacing nationally and internationally produced products with those created locally and regionally

2- Taking responsibility on the effects they have on the natural world

3- Avoid exotic sources of capital for business development and growth

4- Engaging in productive processes that are human, worthy, dignified and intrinsically satisfying

5- Creating objects of durability and long-term utility whose ultimate use or disposition will not be harmful to future generations

6- Changing of consumers to customers through education

7- Promoting transparency and systematic dealings with risks, uncertainty and irreversibility

8- Ensuring appropriate valuation, appreciation and restoration

9- Integrating environmental, social, human and economic goals in business policies and activities

10- Promoting and implementing Continuous Quality Improvement

11- Promoting commitment to the best practices

12- Understanding projects which illustrate the successful application of sustainability principles to business

13- Demonstrating that market forces can drive the company to conduct business in a way that benefits shareholders, society and the environment

14- Integrating sustainability in all business plans

1:01:02- Characteristics of Project Sustainability

1:01:02:01- Adaptability

In organizational management, adaptability is the ability to change something or oneself to fit in occurring changes and to cope with the unexpected disturbances in any environment. In a system it is the ability to adapt itself to efficiently fast enough to changing circumstances. A sustainable project should therefore be open and able to fit in any changing environment or part of a system.

1:01:02:02- Audit ability

An audit is often an evaluation of a person, organization, system, process, enterprise, project or product. But this concept also applies to project management, quality management and for energy conservation. Audits are performed to ascertain the validity and reliability of information in order to express an opinion on something under evaluation and to provide a system of internal control. Because of increasing regulations and need for operational transparency, risk-based audits are being adopted by organizations to cover multiple regulations and standards in order to ensure credibility, good governance and sustainability.

1:01:02:03- Implement ability
One fundamental principle in project management is that it should realistic, feasible, attainable and above all implementable in order for it is sustainable in the market place.

1:01:02:04- Scalability
Scalability deals with the ability of a project to accommodate additions to its capacity or capabilities and expand its scope of operation. It also deals with its ability to increase in size, volume, quantity or scope to accommodate unforeseen additional components or features of the project.

1:01:02:05- Extensibility
This is the ability to extend the project through the addition of new functions or modification of existing functions to effect change while minimizing existing project functions.

1:01:02:06- Maintainability
A project is sustainable when defects can be corrected, it is able to meet new requirements, future maintenance is made easier and it can cope with the changing environment.

1:01:02:07- Manageability
A sustainable should have an organizational structure specifying roles and responsibilities and duties. This will facilitate the management of the project and enhance its sustainability.

1:01:03- Measurement of Project Sustainability

Sustainability is an integrated process involving social, economic, cultural, legal, political, health, environmental, financial and a host of other factors which can facilitate continuity and sustainability of an organization, system, structure or institution in a marketplace.

Sustainability in project operations is measured by:

- Financial capital-these are total financial resources for the project
- Manufacturing capital- this comprise all equipment,
- Natural capital- this refers to land and natural resources
- Human capital- all professional and experts employed
- Social desirability- needed by the society
- Cultural acceptability- it should not violate certain cultural values and norms
- Economic sustainability- able to withstand competition and exist for long
- Technical feasibility- able to be attained or implemented
- Political expediency- in compliance with government rules and regulations
- Operational viability- should be productive
- Environmentally rebuts- positive impact on the environment

Projects that improve the environment will not contribute to sustainable growth unless they also achieve improvement in economic and social measures of progress. A new product, manufacturing process or communication technology can add value to society and the quality of life by improving hygiene or food safety, contributing to the eradication of diseases, reducing occupational diseases and injuries, providing transportation or housing to people at lower costs or broadening access to services such as the internet and other mass media services.

1:01:04- Social Sustainability Performance Metrics

- Paid taxes
- Labor law compliance
- Employee health and safety
- Training and education
- Human Rights
- Community Relationships
- Product responsibility

1:01:05- Project Sustainability Performance Metrics

Generally, projects driven by sustainable growth produce measurable bottom line benefits such as:

- Improvement in productivity
- Product performance in the market
- Market access
- Innovations in product design and function
- Increased rate of return on investment
- Reduced manufacturing costs

1:02- PROJECT MANAGEMENT

Project Management is the art of directing and coordinating human and material resources to achieve stated objectives within limits of time, budget and stakeholders satisfaction. This is often accomplished through the interaction of Project Management elements applied in various phases of the Project Cycle. These project elements include project requirements, organizational options, project team, project planning, opportunities and risks, project control, project visibility, project status, corrective action and project leadership. A project is a human effort that is unique, creates changes, has a defined start and end date, is constrained by time, cost and quality requirements and includes staffs of different units, departments, background, experience and competences.

Project management is also the discipline of planning, organizing, securing and managing resources to bring about successful completion of specific project goals and objectives. Project objectives are specific, measurable, feasible, agreed upon, realistic and timely in order to be implementable and sustainable.

Project management has gone through a whole transformation from the early 1900's especially with the advent of technological development. Engineers in the construction, defense and engineering industries pioneered these transformation and invented different software and applications for project implementation. Henry Gantt invented the Gantt chart for project planning and control techniques. The "Critical Path Method" (CPM) was developed as a joint venture between DuPont Corporation and Remington Rand Corporation for managing plant maintenance projects. The "Program Evaluation and Review Technique" (PERT) was developed by Booz-Allen & Hamilton as part of United States Navy's Polaris submarine program. Of late Microsoft Corporate has developed the "Microsoft Office Project" program for project analysis and scheduling.

Generally, project planning and management consists of:

- Determining how to plan
- Developing the scope statement
- Selecting the planning team
- Identifying deliverables and creating the work breakdown structures
- Identifying the activities needed to complete those deliverables and networking the activities in their logical sequence
- Estimating the resource requirements for the activities
- Estimating time and cost for the activities
- Developing the schedule
- Developing the budget
- Risk planning
- Gaining formal approval to begin work

Some examples of projects are:

- Developing a new product or service
- Effecting a change in structure, staffing, or style of an organization
- Designing a new transport vehicle
- Developing or acquiring a new or modified information system
- Constructing a building or facility
- Building a water system
- Running a political campaign
- Implementing a new business procedure or process.

1:02:01-PROJECT LIFE CYCLE:

The Project Management Life Cycle comprises four principal components:
- Project Initiation
- Project Planning
- Project Execution
- Project Closure

1:02:01-1- Project Initiation
- Develop a Business Case
- Undertake a Feasibility Study
- Establish the Project Charter
- Appoint the Project Team
- Set up the Project Office
- Perform Phase Review

1:02:01-2- Project Planning
- Create a Project Plan
- Create a Resource Plan
- Create a Financial Plan
- Create a Quality Plan
- Create a Risk Plan
- Create an Acceptance Plan

- • Create a Communication Plan
- • Create a Procurement Plan
- • Contract the Suppliers
- − Define the Tender Process
- − Issue a Statement of Work
- − Issue a Request for Information
- − Issue a Request for Proposal
- − Create a Supplier Contract
- − Perform Phase Review

1:02:01:3- Project Execution

- • Build Deliverables
- • Monitor and control
- − Perform Time Management
- − Perform Cost Management
- − Perform Quality Management
- − Perform Change Management
- − Perform Risk Management
- − Perform Issue Management
- − Perform Procurement Management
- − Perform Acceptance management
- − Perform Communications Management

1:02:01-4 Project Closure

- • Perform Project Closure
- • Review Project Completion

1:02:02- PROJRCT MANAGEMENT PRINCIPLES

- • Figure out the type of business and concentrate on it
- • Understand customers requirements
- • Prepare a reasonable plan
- • Build a good team with clear vision
- • Track project status and give it wide visibility
- • Use baseline controls

- Write, share and save salient points
- Test the project
- Ensure customer satisfaction
- Be proactive

1:02:03- MAJOR PROJECT ACTIVITIES

1:02:03:01- FEASIBILITY:
- Project Formulation
- Feasibility Studies
- Strategy design
- Project Approval

1:02:03:02- PLANNING AND DESIGN:
- Base Design
- Cost and schedules
- Contract terms
- Detailed planning

1:02:03:03- CONSTRUCTIONS:
- Manufacturing
- Delivery
- Civil Works
- Installation
- Testing

1:02:03:04- TURNOVER AND STARTUP
- Final Testing
- Maintenance

1:02:04- PROJECT MANAGEMENT KNOWLEDGE AREAS:

This describes project management knowledge and practice in terms of their component processes.

- **Project Integration Management**

This describes the processes required to ensure that the various elements of the project are properly coordinated. This consists of project plan development, project plan execution and integration change control.

- **Project Scope Management**

This describes the processes required to ensure that the project includes all work required to successfully complete the project. This involves project initiation, scope planning, scope definition, scope verification and scope change control.

- **Project Time management**

This describes processes involved in the timely completion of projects. This consists of activity definition, activity sequencing, activity duration estimation, schedule development, and schedule control.

- **Project Cost Management**

This describes the processes to ensure that the project is completed within the approved budget. It consists of resources planning, cost estimation, cost budgeting and cost control.

- **Project Quality management**

This describes the processes required to ensure that the project will satisfy the needs for which it was conceived. It consists of quality planning, quality assurance and quality control.

- **Project Human Resources Management**

This describes the processes required to make the most effective and efficient use of the people involved in the project. It consists of organizational planning, staff acquisition and team development.

- **Project Risk Management**

This describes the processes concerned with identifying, analyzing, and responding to project risk. It consists of risk management planning, risk identification, qualitative risk analysis, quantitative risk analysis, risk response planning, and risk monitoring and control.

- **Project Procurement Management**

This describes the processes required to acquire goods and services from outside the performing organizations. It consists of procurement planning, solicitation planning, solicitation, source selection, contract administration, and contract closeout.

- **Project Communication Management**

This describes the processes required to ensure timely and appropriate generation, collection, dissemination, storage, and disposition of project information. It consists of communications planning, information distribution, reporting, and administrative closure.

1:02:05- ROLE AND RESPONSIBILITIES OF THE PROJECT MANAGER

General Role:
- Understanding the requirements of the project and ensuring that they are thoroughly and meticulously documented

- Preparing the project plan with achievable cost, schedule, and performance goals
- Identifying and managing project risks
- Ensuring that the project team is well organized, adequately staffed and working well together
- Mange project cost, schedule, requirements and design baseline so that they are traceable
- Reporting meaningful metrics for cost, schedule, quality and risks
- Conducting regular status and design review
- Ensuring the adequacy of project documentation and testing
- Maintaining meaningful communications amongst project stakeholders
- Managing the project to attain the project goals and achieve stakeholders' satisfaction

Specific Roles:

Initiate:
- Agree on the project result/goal with project owner

Plan:
- Prepare and sign the project sheet
- Prepare the Milestone Plan
- Prepare the Responsibility Chart
- Prepare the Risk and Opportunity Log

Execute:
- Align the project team
- Lead the project team

Control:
- Control budget, scope, and time as agreed upon in the Project Sheet

- Monitor and report changes on the business environment and their impact on the project
- Track effects of changes in other projects on the project
- Communicate
- Risk management-escalate issues when needed
- Propose go and no go decision

Closure:
- Prepare the closing document
- Available to give feedback to functional managers about team members

1:02:06- PROJECTS AND OPERATIONS COMPARED

PROJECTS	OPERATIONS
* Unique, non-repetitive	* Repetitive
* Limited in time and people	* Eternal
* Unbalanced objectives	* Balanced objectives
* Transient mixture of resources	* Homogeneous resources
* Effectiveness	* Efficiency

1:02:07- PROJECT PERFORMANCE METRICS

- Maturity improvement program
- Process compliance metrics
- Organizational effectiveness tracking
- Real-time project performance figures
- Standard presentation formats
- Measured training
- Best-in-class benchmarking
- Track record
- Customer satisfaction metrics
- Project ROI tracking
- Organizational performance tracking

- Integration of Project management standards
- Performance system
- Planning baseline
- Project baseline tracking
- Risk plans/management
- Quantifiable specifications
- Process analysis and improvement metrics

1:02:08- SOME CAUSES OF PROJECT FAILURES

Generally, characteristics of successful projects focus on the satisfaction of stakeholders, meeting project requirements, meeting quality expectations, operating within cost, meeting deadlines, delivering sustained and actual benefits and providing the project team with professional satisfaction and learning. But when this requirements and expectations are not met, the project is often classified as a failure.

According to the Bull Survey (1998), the major criteria of project failures were missed deadlines (75%), budget overruns (55%), poor communication (40%), inability to meet project requirement (37%), breakdown in communication (57%0, lack of planning (39%) and poor quality control (35%).

The major causes of project failure can be graphically represented as follows:

Serial #	CRITERIA	Percentage
1	Bad communication between relevant parties	57%
2	Lack of planning, resources and activities	39%
3	No quality control	35%
4	Milestones not being met	34%
5	Inadequate coordination of resources	29%
6	Cost overruns	26%
7	Progress mismanagement	20%

Serial #	CRITERIA	Percentage
8	Overall poor management	17%
9	Supplier skills overstretched	13%
10	Suppliers under-resourced	12%
11	Insufficient measurable output	11%
12	Inconsistency of suppliers	4%

Source: The Bull Report (1998)

Generally, projects fail because of the following:-

1- Lack of skills and proven approach to project management and risk management
2- Lack of effective engagement with stakeholders
3- Lack of clear links between the project and the organization's key strategic priorities and success metrics
4- Lack of clear senior management and sponsor/donor ownership and leadership
5- Too little attention to breaking development and implementation into manageable steps
6- Lack of understanding of , and contact with the suppliers at senior levels of the organization
7- Lack of effective project team integration between clients, the supplier team and the supply chain
8- Evaluation of proposals often driven by initial price rather than long-term value for money especially during securing business benefits
9- Project not meeting expectation of stakeholders or beneficiaries
10- Lack of change management processes
11- Lack of continuity in project sponsorship
12- Insufficient availability of resources or budget
13- Escalation of critical problems during project implementation
14- Lack of risk planning
15- Rampant schedule delays and missed commitments
16- Project overrun budgets with no end in sight

17- Uncontrolled project scope

18- Unclear project objectives and goals

19- Lack of availability and application of new technology

20- Poor estimation or weak definition of requirements at project planning stage

21- Vendors inability to meet commitments

22- No internal or external quality control and assurance plans

All these are applicable to project in all sectors including retail, banking, insurance, credit, manufacturing, government departments such as education, health, human services, defense, system software, research and development and academic institutions.

1:02:09- Projects, Programs and Portfolio Management Compared

	PROJECTS	PROGRAMS	PORTFOLIOS
SCOPE	Projects have defined objectives. Scope is progressively elaborated throughout the project life cycle	Programs have a larger scope and provide more significant benefits	Portfolios have a business scope that changes with strategic goals of the organization
CHANGE	Project managers expect change and implement processes to keep change managed and controlled	The program manager must expect change from both inside and outside the program and be prepared to manage it	Portfolio managers continuously manage changes in the broad environment
PLANNING	Project managers progressively elaborate high-level information into detailed plans throughout the project life cycle	Program managers develop the overall program plan and create high-level plans to guide detailed planning at component level	Portfolio managers create and maintain necessary processes and communication relative to the aggregate portfolio

	PROJECTS	PROGRAMS	PORTFOLIOS
MANAGEMENT	Project manager manage the project team to meet the project objectives	Program managers manage the program staff and the project managers, they provide vision and overall leadership	Portfolio managers may manage or coordinate portfolio management staff
SUCCESS	Success is measured by product and project quality, timeliness, budget compliance, and degree of customer satisfaction	Success is measured by the degree to which the program satisfies the needs and benefits for which it was undertaken	Success is measured in terms of aggregate performance of portfolio components
MONITORING	Project manager monitor And control the work of producing the products, services or results that the project was undertaken to produce	Program managers monitor the progress of program components to ensure the overall goals, schedules, budgets, and benefits of the program will be met	Portfolio managers monitor aggregate performance and value indicators

Source: PMBOK Guide, Fourth Edition

CHAPTER TWO

2:00- PROJECT SUSTAINABILITY MANAGEMENT (PSM)

The demand for project sustainability has given rise to a new concept called Project Sustainability Management (PSM). This refers to a complex mix of systems, structures, plans, resources, laws, regulations, technologies and other mechanisms put in place for an effective and efficient management of the sustainability process of any project. The Project Sustainability Management process is designed to customize sustainable development project goals and indicators to suit local conditions and priorities and to ensure that project sustainability goals are aligned and traceable to societal goals and objectives.

A Project Sustainability Management system identifies the relevant issues, objectives and performance levels to be met, establishes an ethical framework as the basis for establishing policies, codes of conduct, consults with and maintains dialogue with stakeholders and accounts for the results achieved.

The global principles of sustainable development are:

1- Future: This is concern for the future. This involves various innovations to create and improve for the future, anticipating for what might come, and enabling information through sharing and greater interaction. Innovation also enhances the collection and assimilation of knowledge about new products and processes.

2- Participation: This is the participation of stakeholders in decision making for the project. This requires a lot of education and trust to engage stakeholders and build their capacity to identify issues, include local values and communicate their experiences.

3- Resources: This is the concern for equity in resource consumption and improvement on its use. This requires continuous improvement on ways to identify and manage the resources and seeking new knowledge and information about it.

4- Environment: This is concern for the quality and integrity of the environment and requires the alignment of global standards to local conditions. This involves using various indicators to align project goals with global goals while factoring in local conditions.

2:01- PROJECT SUSTAINABILITY MANAGEMENT PLAN

2:01:01- Program Summary

This is the process of developing specific strategies and action plan to ensure the long-term sustainability of a project. Consideration focuses on a number of resources and competencies- financial, political, administrative, managerial, educational, cultural, social and economic needed for the realization of the project. The S.M.A.R.T (Specific, Measurable, Attainable, Realistic and Timely) technique may be used here to answer some fundamental questions in project design. Generally questions such as:

*who- who does what

*what- what tasks have to be accomplished

*why- reasons or purpose for doing it

*when- establishment of a time frame of activity

*which- identification of requirement and constraints

*where – identification of location

*how – logistics, transportation and communication issues

All these questions are answered to facilitate the evaluation of the goals and objectives of the project.

2:01:02- Program Mission, Vision, Philosophy and Values

- define scope of activities and scale of operation
- Make sure the fit with community needs
- Define clear vision of what is to be achieved

2:01:03- Identification of Stakeholders and Advocates

- Develop a list of sponsors with contact information
- Develop a list of political leaders with contact information
- Develop a list of community leaders and other resource persons

2:01:04- Results Orientation

- Adopt a result framework
- Develop data and use for improvement
- Communicate results to stakeholders
- Define success and failures
- Measure progress and share results
- Develop systems for collecting and analyzing data

2:01:05- Financial Planning and Analysis

- Determine resources needed for the project
- Determine the fiscal needs
- Make the best use of existing resources
- Create partnerships
- Explore national and international revenue sources

2:01:06- Program Adaptation to Changes

- Develop a program to respond to changes in funding and the environment
- Participate in collaborative advocacy to encourage change

- Monitor announced opportunities for funding
- Consider new ways of making improvement

2:01:07- Management Structure

- Recruit a multi-disciplinary team for the project
- Emphasize on professionals with experience
- Try to build a technocratic team
- Assign roles and responsibilities
- Delegate power and authority where and when need be

2:01:08- Support Systems

- Develop fiscal management, accounting, information and personnel systems
- Develop other support system from the community

2:01:09- Program Monitoring and Evaluation

- Develop a check list of sustainability analysis

2:01:10- Program Report Documentation

- Document, save and file all project documents.

2:02- SOME SUSTAINABILITY SOCIETY INDEXES

1- Basic Needs:- Sufficient food, sufficient drinking water, safety, good sanitation, appropriate housing, basic health needs, clothing
2- Personal Development:- Life expectancy and longevity, relationship, educational opportunities, gender equality, employment, strong family ties

3- Well-Balanced Society:- Good governance, equitable income distribution, population growth, justice, security, employment, social amenities, freedom and liberty, balanced development

4- Healthy Environment:- Air quality, surface water quality, quality available food, available health facilities, available healthcare professionals, good environmental hygiene

5- Climate and Energy:- Consumption of renewable energy, emission of Greenhouse gases control, pollution control

6- Natural Resources:- Use of renewable water resources, forest protection and Conservation, mineral resource exploitation control, endangered species control
And Biodiversity

7- Preparation for the Future:- Material consumption, organic farming, strategic planning, savings and investment

8- Economy:- Gross Domestic Product (GDP), Per Capita Income (PCI), Consumer Price Index (CPI), inflation, employment, Public Debt

2:03- PROJECT SUSTAINABILITY MANAGEMENT CHECKLIST

1- Continuous Quality Improvement (CQI)

The basic principle in CQI is to seek to increase probability of desired project outcomes, assess and improve processes involved in project activities that processes are carried out by all staffs that people do unintentionally make mistakes and that undesirable project outcomes can be avoided if processes are improved. The outstanding features of CQI are that it is proactive; process-focused, follow functional lines, seeks continued improvement and requires responsibility of all employees.

2- Project Periodic Updates

Encouraging and supporting clients, customer, sponsors and stakeholders to incorporate sustainability in statements and requirements and application throughout the project cycle

3- Project Team selection:
Incorporating sustainability criteria into selection of team members, contractors, suppliers, their credentials and various specialists involved in the implementation of the project.

4- Project Strategies
This requires considering sustainability as the fundamental options of scoping, phasing, sequencing, sourcing, procurement, contracts etc.

5- Project legislation
Identifying the current legislation (laws, rules and regulations, ordinances etc) and standards and how to comply with them

6- Project Financing
This is devising business benefits, securing monetary incentives, avoiding taxes, penalties and charges that can derail the goals and objectives of the project.

7- Project Change Management
This is addressing sustainability aspects when change is under review in order to make tactical decisions for the project

8- Project Risk Management
This is the evaluation of all the risk factors and impact on the sustainability of the project.

9- Project Deliverables
This is reviewing, updating, confirming, promoting and imple-menting the predetermined project sustainability arrangements, corporate standards and good governance practices, including waste avoidance, packaging and sequencing effectiveness

10- Project Communication Channels

This involves the facilitation of all forms of communication (written, verbal, electronic etc) with all staffs, stakeholders, sponsors and the community.

11- Project Quality Assurance (QA)

These are activities directed towards assuring quality of products and service,

Identification of important aspects of care, establishment of thresholds or benchmarks (eg.100%), monitoring Performance, identification of Problems, correction of problems, evaluation of effectiveness of systems (i.e., Continuous Monitoring).

CHAPTER THREE

3:00- SUSTAINABLE PROCESS DEVELOPMENT

The quality improvement process involves planning, organizing and monitoring. This process can, of course, be represented by a flowchart. The way it looks and is done may vary depending on organizational procedures and resources. The objective is the same: to identify problems in processes, thereby preventing compromises in quality in the products or services delivered to customers. It is easier to continue to do things as they always have been done than to scrutinize processes. This is true even when we know there are wasteful, annoying or problematic steps in a process. Processes must be managed and improved. This involves:

- Defining the process,
- Measuring process performance (metrics),
- Reviewing process performance,
- Identifying process shortcomings,
- Analyzing process problems,
- Making a process change,
- Measuring the effects of the process change,
- Communicating between employees, supervisors and management.

Total Quality Management offers a process for looking at and improving processes. TQM not only challenges us to change, but provides the tools to facilitate it. These tools focus attention on the way we do things rather than what we accomplish. One tool or technique is to ask the six questions all journalism students are taught to use such as Who, What, Where, Which, When, Why and How.

Throughout the steps of planning, organizing and monitoring processes to achieve improvement, these questions are essential. A scientific approach to quality issues is central to TQM. Identification of needs and evaluation of the impact of implemented changes are database. Facts and figures allow easy comparison of "before" and "after." Only the measurement of improvements can prove the effectiveness of changes. Just as quality improvement uses a process-oriented model, problem solving is most easily conceptualized and realized as a process. However, while quality improvements involve focusing on an entire process, problem solving is related to a single area where things are 'stuck." Identification and resolution of the problem is necessary before things can continue. This is often achieved through Process Flow Analysis using Process Flow Charts. In this process, various activities in a project or program are identified and analyzed and evaluated for the most cost-effective, efficient and qualitative method of operation. There are then arranged in a sequence according to how they have to be implemented. This is often in a configuration management format on a floe chart.

Traditionally, management responds to issues, conflicts and defects by reacting to information which is provided (without gathering additional data), assuming causes and fixing the problem. Problem-solving with TQM entails clear steps including recognition, identification and evaluation of possible causes and solutions, selection of a solution to address a specific cause, implementation and monitoring-all accomplished through use of scientific approaches and statistical tools. While these steps may occur in an orderly sequence, the process allows for returning to steps to gain clarification and directions.

THE TQM PROCESS

PLANNING- Vision, mission and strategic planning

IMPLEMENTATION- Information and analysis, human resources and organizational development, process management

RESULTS- Customer satisfaction, financial analysis, competitive advantage, work process improvement

FACTORS AFFECTING PROCESS IMPROVEMENT

INPUTS- Raw materials, data, supplies, training

RESOURCES-
Human- knowledge, skills and experience, people
Physical-site, plant and equipment
Mechanical-machines and computers

CONTROLS-
Internal- procedure, standards and capacity;
External- Regulators, Legislators and requirements

OUPUTS- Products and services, information, paperwork

INTERNAL AND EXTERNAL CUSTOMERS

INTERNAL CUSTOMERS- Peers, leaders, other divisions and departments within the organization

EXTERNAL CUSTOMERS- Community, National, state, county and local governments, business and industry, consumers or end users

3:01- PROCESS FLOW CHART

A flow chart is a pictorial representation describing a process being studied or used to plan the stages of a project. It provides people with a common language or reference point when dealing with a project or process. Flow charts provide an excellent form of documentation for a process and are useful when examining how various steps in a process work together. The American National Standards Institute (ANSI) established its own symbols, which are used to analyze the second condition of a flow chart process.

Flowcharting is a graphic representation of a series of steps that are performed in a specific work process. The important uses of Flowcharting are:

- Identifying the actual path that a product or service follows to show redundancies, inefficiencies and misunderstandings,
- Creating a common understanding of the work process,
- Identifying customers previously neglected,
- Identifying opportunities for improvement,
- Identifying the ideal path for a product or service,
- Setting boundaries.

GENERAL PROCESS PROCEDURE

Generally, process development and management has a sequence for information input, processing and generating results or output. The process flow can be represented as follows:

CHART 3:01

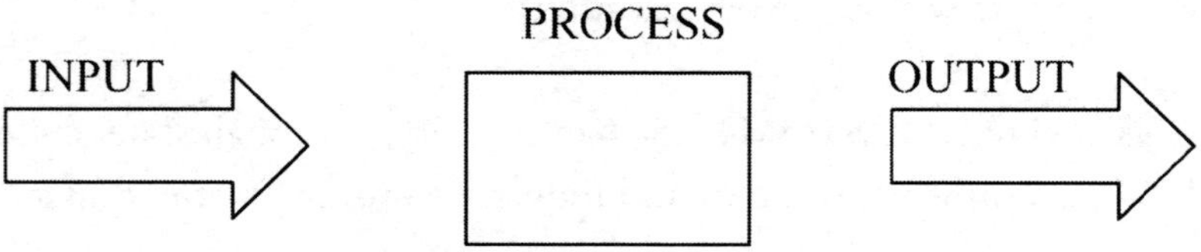

PROCESS

INPUT ⟹ [   ] OUTPUT ⟹

CHART: 3:02- PROCESS FLOW CHART SYMBOLS

A flowchart contains symbols to identify activities or sequential steps beginning, end and decision points; connections or relationships; and the direction or path, which is followed in the process.

Start or end of the program

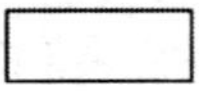

Computational steps or processing function

Input or output Operation

Decision Making and Branching

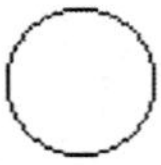

Connector or joining of two parts of the program

Magnetic tape

Magnetic Disk

Off-page Connector

← → ↑ ↓ Flow Line

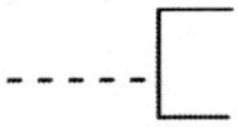

Annotation

Flowchart symbols help to describe various activities in process development,

The Processing or Activity symbol is a description of the activity it represents. The Decision symbol represents a point in the process where a decision or question arises. From there, the process branches into two or more paths depending on the answer that appears. The terminal symbol identifies the beginning or end of a process. The Connector shows a viewer that the diagram continues on another page. Overall, the flowchart helps in the analysis and evaluation of activities to identify inefficiencies, unnecessary loops, process breakdown and opportunities for simplification and improvement.

3:02- TOTAL QUALITY MANAGEMENT TOOLS

These are statistical methods for analyzing numerical data and focusing on results.

3:02:01-Affinity Diagrams

Hierarchical groups of language data with similar thoughts and ideas are sorted together in columns and groups. The purpose is to find missing information such as problems, causes, ideas, solutions and customer requirements.

Data collection process needs	Pressure for success	Lack of follow up by management

Want to solve problems	Lack of training	Unrealistic allotment of time

3:02:02- Tree Diagrams

This is used to find missing categories of information in a structure, usually an organizational chart. It is very useful for identifying probabilities. This should be top-to-bottom vice versa.

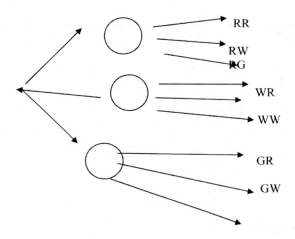

3:02:03- Matrix Diagrams

This defines the levels of relationships between two groups of factors. It helps to visualize and simplify the complex relationships between two groups of factors.

Tanyimor Foundation Inc.	DATA	FUNCTION	NETWORK
SCOPE			
BUSINESS MODEL			
SYSTEM MODEL			
TECHNOLOGY MODEL			
FUNCTIONING ENTERPRISE			

3:02:04- Gantt Charts

This represents a graphical schedule for each task, action or activity necessary to achieve a target or purpose. It is a graphical representation of the duration of tasks against the progression of time. It is useful for project planning and scheduling and for monitoring project progress.

TASK	DURATION	January	February	March
1	1 Week			
2	1 Week			
3	1 Week			
4	1 Week			
5	1 Week			
6	1 Week			

3:02:05- Relationship Diagrams

It shows the degree of drive or influence of a cause on an effect. This determines the cause and effect relationships between many issues so as to visualize logical patterns within them.

3:02:06- Process Decision Charts

It outlines problems and barriers to a predetermined outcome and the corrective actions to be taken if the problems and barriers occur.

3:02:07- Cause and Effects Charts

This can sometimes be displayed using a fishbone and this organizes factors and variables that potentially impact quality, causes of problems and obstacles to the achievement of goals

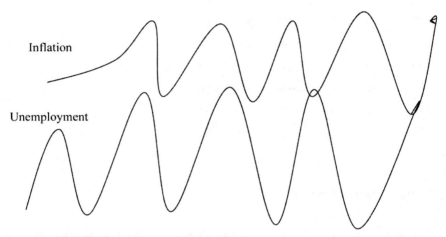

Inflation

Unemployment

Increased inflation increases unemployment

3:03- TOTAL QUALITY MANAGEMENT STATISTICAL TOOLS

Total Quality Management relies on data collection and analysis for objective decision-making. The graphic display of data through statistical tools such as charts and graphs makes it easy to see and understand current status, variations, relative importance of factors, and effectiveness of changes compared to desired impact.

Although there are a wide variety of statistical tools available, including the flowchart, the following six are used most frequently within the quality improvement process: Pareto chart, run chart, control chart, scatter diagram, histogram, and the pie chart. A basic understanding of how to develop and use these tools is needed to implement TQM.

3:03:01- Data Sheets

This is data entry in a table of rows and columns or on single cards. It helps to organize, manage and track data and to calculate relationships between data.

125	0.2	15	21	5	15
130	0.3	20	26	10	20
135	0.5	25	31	15	25
140	0.6	30	36	20	30
145	0.8	40	41	25	35
150	0.7	45	46	30	40

3:03:02- Pareto Charts

This derives its name from the Pareto Principle, which states that 805 of the effects come from 20% of the causes. The chart is a series of vertical bars with their heights reflecting the frequency, cost or impact of the problems.

The data points drawn as proportionally sized bars and ranked by size with or without a line indicating cumulative total with the addition of each item.

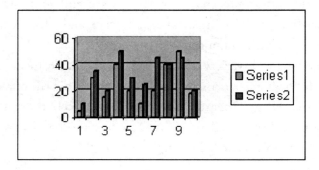

3:03:03- Bar Charts

This represents data points drawn as proportionally sized, side-by-side or stacked bars. It helps to compare distinct non-continuous items.

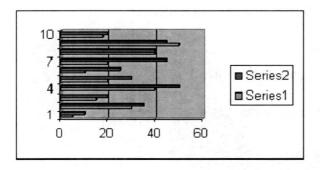

3:03:04- Run Charts

Run charts are also known as trend charts and used to measure change over time. It shows trends, cycles and deviations and illustrates good and bad situations in a process.

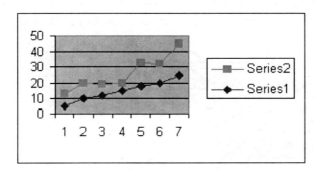

3:03:05- Pie Charts

These are graphical display of relative magnitudes or frequencies of data categories. They help to visualize the proportions and relative importance of contributing items and clearly show frequencies, place, or other data classification, which represents the largest share.

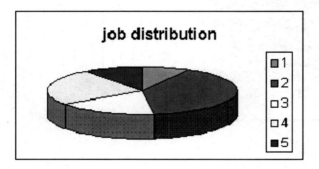

3:03:06- Histograms

This is also called a bar chart or graph and displays variation or distribution of measured data it compares distribution, determines means and modes, and identifies population control limits, mixtures, abnormality or errors.

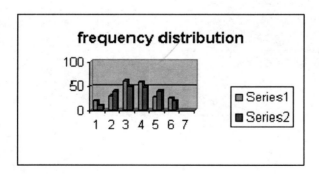

3:03:07- Scatter Diagrams

These are also known as scatter gram or correlation charts and show the relationship between variables. It helps to analyze the correlation between two variables. And to predict future relationships based upon past correlations.

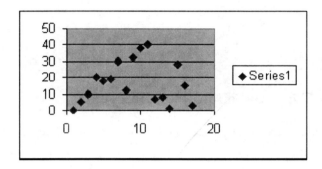

3:03:08- Control Charts

A control chart is used to track important conditions over time and also to indicate the range of variation in a system or process. They are used for continuous values such as length, weight or concentration. Control charts determine whether process characteristics consistently approach extreme control limits. They also determine whether a process is in or out of control.

CHAPTER FOUR

4:00- SUSTAINABLE ORGANIZATIONAL STRUCTURE

A classic sustainable quality organizational structure can be represented as follows:

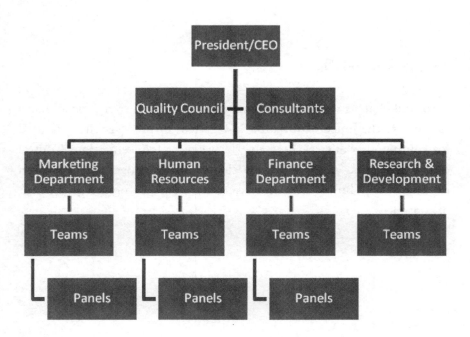

4:01- STRUCTURE

The essential element for a successful quality program is the development of an organizational structure that will institute, sustain and facilitate the expansion of the Total Quality Management process. The quality structure consists of three distinct elements, (the Quality Council, Panels and the Quality Improvement Teams), all supported by a Quality Planning and Development Division. But the key factor here is the alignment among various organizational systems such as human resource systems, including job design, selection processes, compensation and rewards, performance appraisal, training and development that must align and support the new TQM culture. Another system consideration is that TQM should evolve from the strategic plan and be based on stakeholder expectations.

4:01:01- The Executive Council- its main functions are: -

- o Creating the strategic vision
- o Developing the philosophy
- o Promoting and championing the vision
- o Establishing the TQM culture

4:01:02- The Quality Council
The Quality Council consists of a leader (i.e. the Executive Director) and the senior functional managers. The major responsibilities of the Quality Council are:

- Developing and implementing policy.
- Developing and implementing the TQM organizational plan.
- Creating and sustaining TQM teams.
- Overseeing regulations and financial responsibilities.
- Recommending training.
- Facilitating communication.
- Removing barriers that inhibit progress with quality improvements.
- Ensuring the organization's vision is promoted and implemented.

4:01:03- TQM Panels

The functions of Panels in a Total Quality Management implementation process can be summarized as follows:

- Identifying process improvement areas.
- Reviewing process improvements.
- Consulting with TQM teams.
- Coordinating with the Division of Quality Planning and Development.
- Reviewing requests for process improvement opportunities.
- Setting thresholds for evaluations.
- Reviewing performance against thresholds.
- Determining on-going M & E's based team recommendations.

4:01:04:00- QUALITY MANAGEMENT TEAMS

Teams are the focus of activity in Total Quality Management. The success of a team depends on the clarity of its mission, defined decision-making process, openly established and accepted ground rules, education in problem-solving methods, contribution of its members, optimism about outcome and the supportive nature of members to the teams goals and dedication for its success, cooperative relationship, constructive behaviors, enthusiasm, congruity, common purpose, progressiveness and openness.

The two main types of Quality Improvement Teams are cross -Functional and Department Teams.

4:01:04:01-CROSS-FUNCTIONAL TEAMS

Cross-functional Teams represent an exciting and innovative way of solving problems and dealing with issues that affect large portions of an organization. Cross-functional quality improvement team members are selected from several work units, since the problem they will be given affects many areas of the organization, not just one department. Each cross-functional team consists of 6-8 members who work on a specific problem to completion in approximately 3-6 months. These teams, through the application of the principles and tools of TQM, will analyze the given process, collect data, recommend process improvements, implement the improvements and report the findings.

4:01:04:02- DEPARTMENTAL TEAMS

A Department Process Improvement Team follows the same procedure as a Cross-Functional Team when solving an identified problem, but with one major difference: Departmental Teams are concerned with department issues. These teams, regardless of how you chose to label them, need to be differentiated from the Cross-Functional and Departmental Quality Improvement Teams. Self-managed teams can have as many as 30 members, are on-going, work in or on a specific job or task, are accountable for the entire team's work and manage themselves to the extent designated by their supervisors.

Although there may be times when a self-managed team uses the more structured process of a TQM team, most of their efforts are directed toward day-to-day decisions involving projects and changes within their specific unit. In other words, they will rarely need to use the more involved procedures outlined in this handbook.

Regardless of your type of team, it is important to learn and practice good team building skills, and it is also important to keep accurate records and to fulfill your other administrative responsibilities so that your team's success (and difficulties) can be used to help your entire organization. After all, the purpose of quality teams is to find ways to make the organization more effective so that, in turn, everyone from customers to employees to stockholders reaps the benefits.

4:02- TEAM ROLES AND RESPONSIBILITIES

TQM Process Teams are composed of a Team Leader, Team Facilitator and Team Members. TQM teams generally have 6-8 members who have been given one specific process to improve. Teams generally meet weekly and complete their task within a 3-6 month period.

4:02: 01- TEAM LEADER

The role of the Team Leader is to guide the team through the process improvement structure to achieve a successful outcome. The Team Leader conducts the meeting, coordinates arrangements, instructs team members in the process, ensures proper documentation and interfaces with Quality Council, consultants, etc. In other words, the team leader provides direction and focus on the team's activities.

4:02: 02- TEAM FACILITATOR

The role of the Team Facilitator is to promote effective group dynamics so the team can achieve its goal. The team facilitator's specific responsibilities consist of synthesizing ideas, mediating and resolving conflicts, getting honest responses from all members, assisting with training and providing feedback to the team. The facilitator must be a person who does not have a vested interest (or responsibility) in the process being improved. He or she must also be capable of remaining objective with each member. The facilitator must be skilled in the quality tools, techniques and structure, as well as group processes. For Further information regarding this important role, see Section III of this handbook.

4:02:03- TEAM RECORDER

The recorder's role is to capture the basic ideas of the group, usually writing on boards in full view of members. He remains neutral and unbiased.

4:02:04- TEAM MEMBERS

The role of Team Members is to share knowledge and expertise by participating fully in the improvement process. Major responsibilities include participating in all meetings, recognizing that serving on a team is part of one's real job, adhering to the team's ground rules, performing outside team assignments, serving as timekeeper or recorder, as requested, and implementing recommendations. Team Members are an integral part in the organizational quality implementation program. Therefore, commitment is a key work for all team members. Without responsibility and committed team members, the team's goal (and the organization's goal) will not be achieved.

4:03- TRADITIONAL MANAGEMENT AND INTEGRATED MANAGEMENT (TQM) COMPARED

4:03:01-TRADITIONAL MANAGEMENT:

In this approach TQM never becomes an accepted reality by either organization or human resource management. It is usually seen as a competing force or "something to be tolerated". This approach represents 80% failure of TQM implementation. The TQM system consumes valuable resources needed by the other systems and rejection begins to occur. Some of the characteristics of traditional management are:

1. Authoritative Management- the Director takes decision without consulting any lower authorities. .
2. Competition is discouraged- career enhance is not emphasized to avoid other people climbing the corporate ladder.
3. Communication flows in one direction- from the top to the bottom- with an authoritative management style information is disseminated generally from the director to lower authorities and not vice versa
4. Product and service design are dictated by managers- most workers are like "assembly line" workers who are just there to implement decisions. There is no opportunity for suggestions or change in workflow dictated by the higher authority.

5. Decisions are based on assumptions- the management does not often analyze and evaluate situations before taking decisions. It is always assumed that everything will be accomplished.

6. Quality assurance is based on inspection and fixing problems- traditional management does not take a preventive approach to certain problems because it is assumed that all projects will materialize.

7. Status-quo is preferred; precedence prevails- most managers in traditional management do not want changes in the administration and so prefer people to stay in positions indefinitely even if they are not productive.

8. Training is non-productive- since changes and career enhancement is not encouraged sometimes they see no need for any form of training in the organization so employees are often are often not very conversant with contemporary issues affecting organizations as well employees benefits.

CHART 4:02- TYPICAL TRADITIONAL MANAGEMENT ORGANIZATIONAL STRUCUTURE

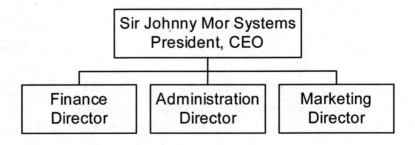

Most traditional management organizational structures are functional and communication and decision-making is mostly vertical-from top to bottom.

4:03:02- INTEGRATED MANAGEMENT (TQM)

In this approach, a Total Quality Management concept is blended and balanced with existing cultural initiatives in both organizational and human resource management systems. This approach represents 20% success of most of TQM implementation. Some of the characteristics of the management approach are:

- Empowered teams direct processes- decisions emanate from panels and teams which are often "cross-functional" and made up of employees from various departments in the organization.
- Trust and collaboration are developed- working in panels and teams makes employees to understand each other better. This helps to create a very trusting relationship among employees.
- Communication flows up, down and horizontal- information flows in all directions in the organization since everyone is involved in decision –making.
- Teams and panels perform product and services designs.
- Panels and teams deliberate on the strategic development and implementation of company goals and objectives.
- Decisions are based on facts and scientific approaches- there is often a lot of analysis and evaluation of facts and figures before decisions are made.
- Quality improvement is based on problem prevention- there is very meticulous planning with provision for maintenance and contingency to avoid irreparable problems
- Innovation, creativity and risk-taking are encouraged- employees are empowered to be original in thought, ingenuous and inventive towards the development of services or products in the organization.
- Investment in training is extremely valuable- there is often a lot of provision for in-service and professional training for clients to acquire the necessary skills and knowledge in order to remain competitive in the market place. Sometimes employees are offered

scholarships to universities for professional studies, which are of benefit to the organization. Tuition re-imbursement also helps employees to complete such professional and academic studies while working.

4:03:03- Differences between Traditional Management and TQM

TRADITIONAL MANAGEMENT	TOTAL QUALITY MANAGEMENT
Authoritative managers supervise departments	Empowered teams direct processes
Competitiveness is rewarded	Trust and collaboration are encourage
Communication flows in one direction, from top to bottom	Communication flows up, down and horizontal
Product and service design and improvement by managers within isolated department	Product and service design and improvement is determined by customers and performed by cross-functional teams
Decisions are based on assumptions and feelings	Decisions are based on facts and scientific approaches
Quality assurance is based on inspection and fixing problems	Quality improvement is based on problem prevention
Status quo is preferred; precedence prevails	Innovation, creativity and risk taking are encouraged
Training is non productive	Investments in training are extremely valuable

CHAPTER FIVE

5:00- STRATEGIC IMPLEMENTATION PLAN (SIP)

This plan is designed to promote and maintain the sustainability for projects and programs in the public, government and non-governmental organizations, multinational organizations, nonprofit organizations, academic and other professional training and development institutions international as well as for individual development and growth. This implementation plan is also beneficial to small and large-scale businesses, agro-industrial complexes, pharmaceutical industries and a host of other businesses needing quality in their products and services as well as their overall operation. This plan contain seventeen important implementation steps which include top management commitment, development of a corporate strategic plan, development of an organizational structure, development of an implementation budget, creation of quality council, teams and panels, starting an awareness plan, training of team leaders and facilitators, conduction of an initial survey, documentation of the implementation plan, quality system documentation, documentation control, actual implementation, internal quality audit, management review, pre-assessment audit, certification and registration and continuous quality improvement.

The implementation of a Sustainability Project Plan affects the entire organization from the start and is pursued with total dedication because it will result in a "paradigm shift" and "cultural transition". The implementation process depends on the sophistication of the society and organization, the size of the organization and the complexity of the process. The basic elements of implementation planning include specifying program goals to be addressed in the identified time period, determining program logic, targeting specific audiences, specifying desired outcomes, determining the current situation, identifying sequenced learning strategies, determining resource needs, and selection of specific marketing, delivery, and evaluation methods. Some of the benefits of effective implementation planning include:

- Opportunities for increased project impact,
- Sequence and continuity in educational programs,
- Clarification of actions and resources needed to implement a program,
- Planned program marketing,
- Improved evaluation and accountability,
- Improved scheduling and management of time and other resources, and
- Greater personal satisfaction through a sense of progress and accomplishment.

During the Establishment Stage, there is planning for leadership training, formation of the executive council, formulation of the philosophy, formation of the quality council, development of the training plan and formation of the quality boards. During the implementation stage too, the assessment of systems occurs, data analysis is ongoing and intervention strategies are being tried. There is also the adoption of the process improvement method and the board and the quality departments begin to assist teams with tools and techniques on an ongoing basis.

The implementation of the Project Sustainability Plan in an organization requires some activities and processes to be carried out for an effective and efficient system operation. Some of these processes are top management commitment, corporate strategic plan, organizational structure, implementation budget, formation of team and panels, awareness programs, training, status surveys, documentation, control, quality audit, management review, certification, registration and continuous quality improvement.

5:01- TOP MANAGEMENT COMMITMENT

Top management notably the President, Minister, Director, Administrator or the Chief Executive Officer of the institution should demonstrate a commitment and a determination to implement the Project Sustainability Management System in the organization. It should also be convinced that registration and certification will enable the organization to demonstrate to its customers a visible commitment to quality and that a quality management system would improve overall business efficiency by the elimination of wasteful duplication in management system. Initially, an orientation is carried out by the Chief Executive Officer (CEO) for all staffs in the health service and conveys the rationale for project sustainability implementation. The basic principles and philosophies of this concept are introduced. This is because Project Sustainability Management is a "paradigm shift", involving a change in culture, thought process, ideas, work habits and professional relationships. This involves moving an organization from a traditional system of operation to a modern one.

Top management should: -

- Communicate the importance of meeting customer as well as statutory and regulatory requirements to the organization,
- Define the organization's quality policy and make it known to every employee,
- Ensure that quality objectives are established at all levels and functions,
- Ensure the availability of resources required for the development and implementation of the quality management system,
- Appoint a management representative to coordinate quality management system activities, and
- Conduct a management review.

Top management should identify goals to be achieved through the quality management system such as being more efficient and profitable, producing products and services that consistently meet customer's needs and expectations, achieving customer satisfaction, increasing market share, improving communication and morale in the organization, reducing costs and liabilities and increasing confidence in the production system.

5:02- DEVELOPMENT OF CORPORATE STRATEGIC PLAN

The corporate strategic plan is the "Blue Print" for the implementation of an organization's vision, goals and objectives, and other activities required fir an effective and efficient production and delivery of products and services. The process is strategic because it involves preparing the best way to respond to the circumstances of the organization's environment, whether or not its circumstances are known in advance; nonprofits often must respond to dynamic and even hostile environments. Being strategic, then, means being clear about the organizations resources, and incorporating both into being consciously responsive to a dynamic environment.

The focus of the corporate strategic plan is on the following:

- Corporate Vision- what the organization wants to be, future products and services concepts and future markets.
- Corporate Mission- how to achieve the corporate vision within a certain time frame, activities to achieve the vision, understanding of top management to line workers, the public, customers and suppliers.

As with any management tool, the strategic plan is used to help an organization do a better job that is to focus its energy, to ensure that members of the organization are working toward the same goals, and to assess and adjust the organization's direction in response to a changing environment. In short, strategic planning is a disciplined effort to produce fundamental decisions and actions that shape and guide what an organization is, what is does, and why it does it, with a focus on the future.

`          ` The process is about planning because it involves intentionally setting goals (i.e., choosing a desired future) and developing an approach to achieving those goals. The process is disciplined in that it calls for a certain order and pattern to keep it focused and productive. The process raises a sequence of questions that helps planners examine experience, test assumptions, gather and incorporate information about the present, and anticipate the environment in which the organization will be working in the future. Finally, the process is about fundamental decisions and actions because choices must be made in order to answer the sequence of questions mentioned above. The plan is ultimately no more, and no less, than a set of decisions about what to do, why to do it, and how to do it. Because it is impossible to do everything that needs to be done in the world, strategic planning implies that some organizational decisions and actions are more important than others- and that much of the strategy lies in making the tough decisions about what is most important to achieving the organizational success. The strategic planning can be complex, challenging and even messy, but it always defined by the basic ideas outlined above- and you can always return to these basics for insight into your own strategic planning process.

1) Strategic Planning and Long-Range Planning:

Although many use these terms interchangeably, strategic planning and long-range planning differ in their emphasis on the "assumed" environment. Long-range planning is generally considered to mean the development of a plan for accomplishing a goal or set of goals over a period of several years, with the assumption that current knowledge about future conditions is sufficiently reliable to ensure the plan's reliability over the duration of its implementation. In the late fifties and early sixties, for example, the U.S. economy was relatively stable and somewhat predictable, and, therefore, long-range planning was both fashionable and useful.

On the other hand, strategic planning assumes that an organization must be responsive to a dynamic, changing environment (not the more stable environment assumed for long-range planning). Certainly a common assumption has emerged in the nonprofit sector that the environment is indeed changeable, often in unpredictable ways. Strategic planning, then stresses the importance of making decisions that will ensure the organization's ability to successfully respond to changes in the environment.

Strategic planning is only useful if it supports strategic thinking and leads to strategic management-the basis for an effective organization. It means making that assessment using three key requirements about strategic thinking: a definite purpose can be in mind; an understanding of the environment, particularly of the forces that affect or impede the fulfillment of that purpose; and creatively in developing effective responses to those forces. It follows, then that strategic management is the application of strategic thinking to the job of leading an organization and this entails attention to the "big picture" and the willingness to adapt to changing circumstances, and consists of the following three elements:

- Formulation of the organization's future mission in light of changing external factors such as regulation, competition, technology, and customers
- Development of a competitive strategy to achieve the mission
- Creation of an organizational structure, which will deploy resources to successfully carry out its competitive strategy.

2) Strategic Planning Model:

Many books and articles describe how best to do strategic planning and many go to much greater lengths than this planning response sheet, but our purpose here is to present the fundamental steps that must be taken in the strategic planning process. Below is a brief description of the five steps in the process. These steps are a recommendation, but not the only recipe for creating a strategic plan; other sources may recommend entirely different steps or variations of these steps. However, the steps outlined below describe the basic work that needs to be done and the typical products of the process.

3) Getting Ready:

To get ready for strategic planning, an organization must first assess if it is ready. While a number of issues must be addressed in assessing readiness, the determination essentially comes down to whether an organization's leaders are truly committed to the effort, and whether they are able to devote the necessary attention to the "big picture". An organization that determines it is indeed ready to begin strategic planning must perform five tasks to pave the way for an organized process:

- Identify specific issues or choices that the planning process should address
- Clarify roles (who does what in the process)
- Create a planning committee
- Develop an organizational profile
- Identify the information that must be collected to help make sound decisions.

4) Articulating Mission and Vision:

A mission statement is like an introductory paragraph: it lets the reader know where the writer is going, and it also shows that the write knows where he or she is going. Likewise, a mission statement must communicate the essence of an organization to the reader. An organization's ability to articulate its mission indicates its focus and purposefulness. A mission statement typically describes an organization in terms of it's:

- Purpose- why the organization exists, and what it seeks to accomplish,
- Business- the main method or activity through which the organization tries it fulfill this purpose,
- Values- the principles or beliefs that guide an organization's members as they pursue the organization's purpose.

Whereas the mission statement summarizes the what, how, and why of an organization's work, a vision statement presents an image of what success will look like. With mission and vision statements in hand, an organization has taken an important step towards creating a shared, coherent idea of what it is strategically planned for.

5) Assessment of the Situation:

Once a service has committed to why it exists and what it does, it must take a clear-eyed look at its current situation. Remember, that part of strategic planning, thinking, and management is an awareness of resources and an eye to the future environment, so that an organization can successfully respond to changes in the environment. Situation assessment therefore means obtaining current information about the organizations strengths, weaknesses, and performance. - Information that will highlight the critical issues that the organization faces and that its strategic plan must address. The Planning Committee should agree on no more than five or to ten critical issues around which to organize the strategic plan. The products of Step Three include:

- A database of quality information that can be used to make decisions; and
- A list of critical issues, which demand a response from the organization.

1) Developing Strategies, Goals, and Objectives:

Once an organization's mission has been affirmed and its critical issues identified, it is time to figure out what to do about them:

a) The broad approaches to be taken (strategies) and
b) The general and specific results to be sought (the goals and objectives). Strategies, goals, and objectives may come from individual inspiration, group discussion, formal decision-

making techniques, and so on- but the bottom line is that, in the end, the leadership agrees on how to address the critical issues. Discussions at this stage frequently will require additional information or a reevaluation of conclusions reached during the situation assessment. It is even possible that new insights will emerge which changes the thrust of the mission statement.

2) Completion of the Written Plan:

The mission has been articulated, the critical issues identified, and the goals and strategies agreed upon. This step essentially involves putting all that down on paper. Usually one member of the Planning Committee, the executive director, or even a planning consultant will draft a final planning document and submit it for review to all key decision makers (usually the board and senior staff). This is also the time to consult with senior staff to determine whether the document can be translated into operating plans (the subsequent detailed action plans for accomplishing the goals proposed by the strategic plan) and to ensure that the plan answers key questions about priorities and directions in sufficient detail to serve as a guide.

5:03- DEVELOPMENT OF AN ORGANIZATIONAL STRUCTURE

A preliminary step in Project Sustainability Management implementation is to assess the organization's current reality. This 'reality check' enables the organization's top management to identify the relevant preconditions to be done with the history; current needs, precipitating events leading to project sustainability and existing employee quality of life. The "Force-Field Analysis" helps in looking at which forces may be strengthened and which restraining forces may be eliminated, mitigated or counteracted. The organization should be healthy with determining factors such as available funds, strong administrative system, good managerial skills and high employee morale.

Desirable preconditions for an effective Project Sustainability Implementation Plan are identified in two areas: macro and micro. Macro factors include those, which are concerned with issues such as leadership, resources and surrounding infrastructure. The leadership should champion new ideas; there should be continuity of political leadership, a healthy civic infrastructure, shared vision and goals by leaders, trust among those in power, available outside resources and models to follow. The micro factors should center on top management support, customer focus, long-term strategic plans, employee recognition and training, employee empowerment and teamwork, measurement and analysis of products and processes and quality assurance. It changes the organization's political system-decision making processes and power bases. Information systems will be redesigned to measure and track new indicators such as service quality. Financial management processes may also need attention through the realignment of budgeting and resource allocation systems. A typical quality organizational structure is often mixed between a functional, project and matrix organizational structures. Various functional departments exist as specialized panels and are horizontally followed by quality improvement teams. Meanwhile outside consultants and mentors interact directly with the executive director, the quality council and the division of quality and planning. A typical quality organizational structure in a health service organization should comprise:

- The Executive Director
- The Quality Council
- Quality Management Consultants and Contractors
- Specialized Panels representing various departments and divisions
- Quality Improvement Teams representing various departments
- Division of Quality and Planning
- Departments-Ongoing monitoring and evaluation.

A good system in Africa should have an organizational structure, which should enable it to better deliver quality effective and efficient services to clients.

5:04- DEVELOPMENT OF IMPLEMENTATION BUDGET

Typical cost considerations are orientation, leadership training, train-the-trainer for selected staffs, facilitator training for selected staffs, off site training for the executive council, off site training for the quality department, general staff training, library materials, training aids and resources, facility costs and consultation. A good budget ensures the sustainability of any good healthcare delivery system.

5:05- QUALITY COUNCIL, TEAMS AND PANELS

The Quality Council consists of the Executive Director, Managers and Directors of the functional departments and divisions. The purpose of this is to manage team and departmental processes as well as results, focus on "how" rather than "who", use team approach to determine decision procedures, base team efforts on solid foundation of data, give responsibilities and accountabilities to team members, measure and monitor team goals and objectives, participate in meetings to achieve organizational goals, evaluate the effectiveness of meetings and develop agenda with team expectations and outcomes. Team and Panel members should include representatives of all units and departments of the organization - Marketing, Planning, Human Resources, Quality Improvement, and Public Relations/Customer Service, Hospital and Ancillary Operations, Financial services, Environmental Services etc.

5:06- STARTING AN AWARENESS PROGRAM

The Project Sustainability Management awareness program is conducted to communicate to employees the aims of the management system, the advantages to employees, customers and the organization, how it will work and their roles and responsibilities in the system. The program should stress the higher levels of participation and self-direction that the quality management system renders to employees.

5:07- TRAINING OF TEAM LEADERS AND FACILITATORS

All professionals need to have ongoing training on various changes and technologies affecting various services in general as well as various techniques, strategies and ethical issues affecting the way they carry out their duties. This training emphasizes the importance of personal and team effectiveness and covers the basic concepts of quality management systems and the standards and their overall impact on the strategic goals and vision of the organization, the changed processes, and the likely work culture implications in the system. Initial training is also required for writing quality manuals, procedures and work instructions, auditing principles, techniques of laboratory management, calibration, testing procedures etc. It takes the individual from dependence to interdependence. Selected staffs are chosen as formal trainers and receive "training of trainers" instruction to edify their understanding of the material and to strengthen their teaching skills. Selected staffs are also chosen as "facilitators" because effective facilitation is integral to team processes to be used widely throughout the organization.

5:08- CONDUCTION OF AN INITIAL STATUS SURVEY

This involves comparing the existing quality management system in the health service with the Project Sustainability Management standard. A "gap analysis" is conducted whereby an organizational flow chart on process development and improvement is established, and documents requiring modification and elaboration should be identified and listed. During this review process, wide consultation with executives and representatives of various departments and divisions is required to enlist their cooperation. Resource people are identified for information gathering and a fairly organized and successful department is selected in order to develop the new system. Once it is approved, it is adapted, supplemented and implemented according to project sustainability standards. This often requires organizational arrangements, the drawing up of additional documents and possible removal of existing documents (e.g. procedures, inspection/test plans, inspection/test instructions) and records (e.g. inspection/test reports, inspection/test certificates).

5:09- DOCUMENTED IMPLEMENTATION PLAN

Once the organization has obtained a clear picture of how its quality management system compares to the Project Sustainability Management standard, all non-conformances must be addressed with a documented implementation plan. Usually the plan calls for identifying and describing processes to make the organization's quality management system fully in compliance with the standard. This involves the quality documentation to be developed, objectives of the system, person or team responsible, approval required, training required, resources required and estimated completion date. All these elements are organized in a detailed flow chart and each plan defining the responsibilities of various departments and personnel and setting target dates for the completion of activities.

5:10- QUALITY SYSTEM DOCUMENTATION

Documentation is very crucial for all medical services because if a service is not documented, then it was not rendered. It helps to protect healthcare professional in case of any eventuality. In the implementation of a Project Sustainability Management strategy, documentation of the quality management system should include documented statements of a quality policy and quality objectives, a quality manual, documented procedures and records required by the standards as well as documents needed by the organization to ensure the effective planning, operation and control of its processes.

5:11- DOCUMENT CONTROL

A documented system must be created to control the quality management system generated. This helps to manage the creation, approval, distribution, revision, storage and disposal of the various types of documentation. Document control should include:

- Approval for adequacy by authorized persons before issue,
- Review, updating and re-approval of documents by authorized persons,
- Identification of changes and the revision status of the documents,
- Availability of relevant versions of documents at point of use,
- Identification and control of documents of external origin,
- Assurance of legibility and identifiably of documents, and
- Prevention of unintended use of obsolete documents.

The principle of Project Sustainability Management document control is that employees should have access to the documentation and records needed to fulfill their responsibilities.

5:12- IMPLEMENTATION

The implementation process of the Project Sustainability Management strategy in any sector of the economy should be monitored to ensure that the quality management system is effective and efficient and conforms to the standard. These activities include internal quality audits, formal corrective action and management review. It is also advisable to evaluate areas where the chances of a positive evaluation are high, to maintain the confidence of both management and staff on the merits of implementing the quality management system.

5:13- INTERNAL QUALITY AUDIT

The effectiveness of the system should be checked by regular internal quality audits as the system is being installed. This helps to verify that the installed management system conforms to the planned arrangements, to the requirements of the Project Sustainability Management standard and to the quality management system established by the organization. This is also to ensure that it is effectively implemented and maintained, and should be planned and performed as part of the ongoing strategy.

5:14- MANAGEMENT REVIEW

An internal audit and management review should be conducted and corrective actions implemented when the installed quality management system has been operating from three to six months. The management reviews are conducted to ensure the continuing stability, suitability, adequacy and effectiveness of the quality management system. The review includes assessing opportunities for improvement and the need for changes to the quality management system, including the quality policy and quality objectives. The input to management review should include information on results of audits, customer feedback, process performance, product conformity, status of preventive and corrective actions, follow-up actions from previous management reviews, changes that could affect the quality management system and recommendations for improvements. Management reviews should also address the pitfalls to effective implementation, lack of executive commitment, failure to involve everyone in the process and the failure to monitor progress and enforce deadlines.

5:15- PRE-ASSESSMENT AUDIT

The pre-assessment audit provides a degree of confidence for formally going ahead with an application for certification as a quality management organization. Normally an independent and qualified auditor is hired for the pre-assessment before applying for certification.

5:16- CERTIFICATION AND REGISTRATION

Once the quality management system has been in operation for a few months and has stabilized, a formal application for certification is made to a certification agency. If the documents conform to the requirements of the quality standard, the on-site audit is carried out. If the certification body finds the system to be working satisfactorily, it awards the organization a certificate of operation for a period of three years. During this period, it will carry out periodic surveillance audits to ensure that the system is continuing to operate satisfactorily.

5:17- CONTINUOUS QUALITY IMPROVEMENT (CQI)

Certification to Project Management standards is not an end. The organization should continually seek to improve the effectiveness and suitability of the quality management system through the use of quality policy, quality objectives, audit results, analysis of data, corrective and preventive actions and management reviews. The basic principle in CQI is to seek to increase probability of desired project outcomes, assess and improve processes involved in project activities that processes are carried out by all staffs that people do unintentionally make mistakes and that undesirable project outcomes can be avoided if processes are improved. The outstanding features of CQI are that it is proactive; process-focused, follow functional lines, seeks continued improvement and requires responsibility of all employees.

The basic concepts behind Continuous Quality Improvement are:

A) Quality in Fact:
- Doing the right thing,
- Doing it the right way,

- Doing it right the first time,
- Doing it on time.

B) Quality in Perception:
- Delivering the right product or service,
- Satisfying customer's needs,
- Meeting customer's expectations,
- Treating customers with dignity, integrity, courtesy and respect.

C) Measurement of Quality:
- Accuracy- whether the target diagnosis or range is hit,
- Precision- how well a procedure produces a value,
- Data plotting techniques (statistical graphs),
- Charts (flow, control, Pareto, histogram, run scatter, pie).

D) Benchmarks of Quality:
- Organization's own standards,
- Utilization Reviews,
- Institutional Standards (e.g. Critical Care Pathways),
- Peer Review/Professional Standards,
- Country Regulations for example Inspections, Proficiency Surveys etc.

E) Quality Control:
- Monitoring elements of care e.g. Instruments and test procedures,
- Testing systems monitored so that the test results are valid,
- Statistics validating test results,
- Focus on performance not test utility,
- Problem-focused not patient-focused,
- Seeks random improvement rather than systematic improvement,
- Follow organizational workflow charts.

F) Quality Assurance:
- Activities directed towards assuring quality of products and services,

- Identification of important aspects of care,
- Establishment of thresholds or benchmarks (eg.100%),
- Monitoring Performance,
- Identification of Problems,
- Correction of Problems,
- Evaluation of Effectiveness of Systems (i.e., Continuous Monitoring).

5:18- SOME BENEFITS OF STRATEGIC IMPLEMENTATION

5:18:01-INDIVIDUAL MANAGEMENT SKILLS:

- Understanding the role of management in contemporary organizations
- Dealing with conflicting needs of management, peers and staffs
- Understand the key components of strategic planning and management
- Evaluation of an organization's strengths and weaknesses and planning for improvement
- Measuring team performance and that of individual staffs
- Conducting effective performance appraisal
- Being cost-effective and time-effective in service delivery
- Setting up and facilitating process improvement teams
- Involving staffs in selecting critical indicators and setting goals
- Problem-solving and decision making tools
- Communicating performance to customers
- Measuring capability to meet customer needs
- Creating teams and measurement systems
- Understanding the importance of customer service
- Training people to improve on performance

5:18:02- ORGANIZATIONAL IMPROVEMENT

- Becoming effective and efficient in organizational leadership and management
- Setting up mission, goals and objectives for the organization
- Identifying indicators that measure benefits to the customer, staffs and stakeholders
- Development of strategic plans that will impact objectives
- Understand the value of strategic planning and management
- Building quality into all processes
- Involving people in the process of continuous improvement
- Working collaboratively with individuals, teams and organizations
- Measuring all key processes
- Dealing effectively with problems
- Simplification of processes
- Making change a way of life.
- Increasing commitment to change and improvement
- Reducing conflicts between departments and individuals

CHAPTER SIX

6:01- TOTAL QUALITY MANAGEMENT FUNDAMENTALS

Total Quality Management (TQM) or Strategic management is a philosophy of total organizational involvement in improving all aspects of the quality of product or service provided by the organization. This concept is achieved through employee empowerment in decision making, the use of facilitated teams in the organization, individual responsibility for products and services, a strong customer service orientation, working from a set of values envisioning a mission, maintaining commitment, sustaining motivation, prioritizing tasks, cooperating and collaborating with others, communicating effectively and efficiently and seeking to continuously learn and grow. The definition of TQM can be further elaborated as follows:

TOTAL-The responsibility of achieving quality lies on everyone and it recognizes the need to develop processes across the business that will deliver desired customer services and goods according to their requirements with the most cost-effective strategy and maximum return on investment.

QUALITY- The cardinal objective and goal of any business is to attain the highest level of quality in product and service delivery to satisfy the needs of the customer. Product or services have to be delivered at the right time, place and price in order to retain the customers and remain competitive and sustainable in the market place.

MANAGEMENT- Top management must lead the drive to attain quality for its customers by effectively and efficiently communicating the business philosophy, vision, goals and objectives to all employees and internal and external customers and promoting the continuous quality improvement culture.

The first application of management theory took place in non-profits and government agencies and the first conscious and systematic application of this management principle was in the reorganization of the US Army in 1901. The identification of management with business began with the Great Depression of 1929and continued throughout the Second World War, and became more intensified after the war during the period of reconstruction.

The concept of Total Quality Management has grown out of the work of several individuals who have studied and developed models for personal and organizational effectiveness and improvements. These individuals include Dr. W. Edwards Deming, Stephen Covey, Joseph Juran and Philip Crosby who professed that unfaltering commitment by all is essential for an effective and efficient implementation of an organization's philosophy, goals and objectives. Isolated examples of excellence are not the goal, but system-wide quality. This requires providing training to everyone, not only in his or her areas of expertise, but also in the areas of personal responsibility, leadership and improvement progress. These individuals were later sent to Japan by the US State Department to help in the reconstruction of the Japanese economy badly devastated by the bombings during the war. The Japanese easily embraced the TQM concept and it quickly revolutionized their economy and that remains one of the greatest turning points in Japanese economic miracle. Throughout its industrial recovery and take-off in the late 1940's and the 1950's, Japanese industries such as Sony, Yamaha, Suzuki, and Toyota etc have all implemented the TQM concept and it has tremendously helped in the enhancement of the quality of its goods and services. Japanese companies now have affiliates and franchises in almost every country around the globe with available experts for customer service and other necessary assistance.

The term Total Quality Management was first introduced in Great Britain in 1983 by the Trade and Industry Department of Margaret Thatcher's government when it launched its quality campaign. It is a proven method of reaching the goal of quality. This is a leadership system that responds to customers while creating and maintaining an organization culture that values involvement and continuous efforts to improve quality. It is a philosophy that includes learning to apply the necessary techniques, tools and viewpoints that allow organizations to keep customers and maintain a positive rewarding work environment for employees.

The underlying principles of Total Quality Management have been stated in many ways, but they include the basic ideas of working from a set of values envisioning a mission, maintaining commitment, sustaining motivation, prioritizing tasks, cooperating with others, communicating effectively, and seeking to continuously learn and grow. By putting these ideas into practice, individuals and organizations achieve significant and readily apparent benefits for themselves and others. The basic concept behind TQM is that it is very expensive to maintain quality by inspections, and much more efficient to build quality products in the first place. As a result, the responsibility for quality is placed with the workers who actually produce the products. Quality control departments are therefore refocused on different responsibilities, such as training employees in quality control, conducting audits of the quality of the company's parts and suppliers, making final test of finished goods and implementing quality control concepts throughout the company. There are many aspects to TQM such as employee empowerment in decision- making, the use of teams in organization, individual responsibility for products or services, and strong customer service orientation.

Total Quality Management is intended to result in the improvement of services and products not by looking at what is produced but by examining the process for root causes of problems, defects and errors. Total Quality Management relies on the development of personally effective individuals committed to a common vision and an emphasis on customer needs and perceptions. It is based on scientific approaches to decision making, using sequential steps to gather and analyze information in an objective manner and monitoring and evaluating processes with data and statistical tools. Another important feature of TQM is the shift in focus from the end product or service to the processes involved. By focusing on how something is done, rather than what is accomplished, quality can be most dramatically impacted, which ultimately results in improved products and services.

TQM is not a simple solution to quality problems or management issues, but it is an effective one. TQM usually demands cultural changes within the organization because it is a different system to be added to the already existing traditional organizational structures and paradigms. Modern corporate management now has to focus on the long-term, market orientation, a participative management culture, process control and a commitment to continuously improve all products and services. These prerequisites all fall within the general category of principles and practices of Total Quality Management (TQM), Total Quality Control (TQC), and Continuous Quality Improvement (CQI). Companies vary in how they describe the TQM environment, for example Texas Instruments describes its comprehensive management model as having five interrelated components: customer first, teamwork, management by fact, excellence, and policy deployment. Hewlett-Packard describes its Total Quality system as including four cornerstones: customer focus, planning, process management, and an improvement cycle. With the adoption of TQM in 1989, the National Society for Professional Engineers (NSPE) with its 250 projects knew that this meant that their organization was customer-focused; process-oriented, and committed to continuous improvement.

While implementation of TQM may yield immediate, visible improvement, the goal is not to quick-fix things but to develop relationships and processes capable of generating and sustaining quality improvement now and in the future. For the 21st century corporate world, social contracts will be essential because they link employees to employer, and because the natural responsibility of employees arise from social contracts based on trust by employers and employees. The employee invests his resources in the organization and the organization owes individuals investment in term of development job experience, education, salary and supportive and conducive environment.

6:02- TOTAL QUALITY MANAGEMENT AND THE PARADIGM SHIFT

Paradigms are a way that we perceive and understand the world and understanding the power of paradigms is vital to personal effectiveness and growth. The paradigms we embody can be enlightening, allowing us to experience new and wonderful things, but can just be as blinders that shield us from new thoughts or experiences. We need to change and update what is around us-make paradigm shifts. The power of shifting paradigms is all around us, but so is the failure that results when we are resistant to change. So is the TQM process. Recognizing and understanding the power of our personal paradigms and those of our organizations is very important for us to adjust to organizational changes. Personal computers, fax machines, cellular phones, automated banking machines, solar-powered calculators, laser printers, anti-lock automobile brakes, compact discs and digital video disc (DVD) players are all items that would be unthinkable a few years ago. This been a great paradigm shift in the lives of individual and organizations.

6:03- PRINCIPLES OF TOTAL QUALITY MANAGEMENT

Total Quality Management has certain underlying principles guiding its efficient and effective implementation.

In a TQM environment, employees use special techniques to capture the voice of the customer, identify and eliminate the root cause of problems, and control unwanted process variation. It integrates the customer information system, complaint handling system, suggestion system, and objective setting system. The new global leaders will be people who can transmit knowledge and power to each member of an organization. This is a total paradigm shift and Total Quality Management responds to this. Successful Total Quality Management requires both behavioral and cultural changes. The organizational management system, human resource management system and the total quality management system must be aligned in a successful TQM initiative. In general, the Total Quality Management environment is built around a specific set of principles, tools, techniques and systems.

The basic principles of Total Quality Management are:

- Quality can and must be managed
- Everyone has a customer and is a supplier
- Processes, not people are the problem
- Every employee is responsible for quality
- Problems must be prevented, not just fixed
- Quality must be measured
- Quality improvement must be continuous
- The quality standard is defect-free
- Goals are based on requirements, not negotiations
- Life cycle costs, not front end costs
- Management must be involved and lead
- Plan and organize for quality improvement

The 21st century workplace will be totally different from what we have now, and its members must be aligned with and own strategic direction of the business, have trust-based work relationships, and be able to build value with one another and their customers. This is the concept of Total Quality Management, or TQM. Leadership in the TQM workplace has to be seen not as a job, based on power and authority, but as a function based on principles, new people skills, and the ability to engage others in coming to consensus around critical decisions and problem solving. This resulting trust and productivity will provide the enterprise a clear competitive advantage.

TQM has its roots in America and many of its elements are rooted in theories and practices of management that were developed in the USA. Problems arise primarily from imperfect processes, not from imperfect people. Industrial experience has shown that 85% of all problems are process problems that are solvable by managers, with the remaining 15% being problems requiring the action and improvement of performance of individual workers. This principle is popularly known as the "85/15 Principle". Thus quality problems are primarily management problems because only management has the power to change work processes. Schmidt and Finnigan (1992) suggest that TQM's roots include: -

- o Scientific Management - Finding the best way to do a job,
- o Group Dynamics - Enlisting and organizing the power of group experience,
- o Training and Development - Investing in human capital,
- o Achievement Motivation - People getting satisfaction from accomplishment,
- o Employee Involvement - Workers should have some influence in the organization,
- o Socio-Technical System - Organizations operating as open systems,
- o Organization Development - Helping organizations to learn and change
- o Corporate Culture - Beliefs, myths, and values that guide the behavior of people throughout the organization,
- o The New Leadership Theory - Inspiring and empowering others to act,
- o The Linking-Pin Concept of Organization - Creating cross-functional teams,
- o Strategic Planning - Determining where to take the organization and how and when to get there.

According to William P. Anthony (1996), TQM is a strategic and integrated system of management for achieving satisfaction that involves managers and employees and uses quantitative methods to continuously improve quality. This concept continued to sweep across corporate America in the 1970's. This led to a mad rush of small and medium sized companies into it, as well as giant companies, such as General Motors, ICI, and British Petroleum. Michele L. Bechtell (1995) outlines some basic principles, which describe some basic practices associated with the school of Total Quality Management such as aligning the organization's goals with change in the environment, focusing on the vital few strategic traps, working with others to develop plan to close the gaps, specifying the methods and measures to achieve the strategic objectives and making visible the causes and effective linkages among local plans and continuously improving the planning process.

Bechtel, Michele (1995), states that the standardized problem-solving methodology from the school of Total Quality Management is a logical common sense method of solving any type of problem, and that the problem-solving process provides a road map to help senior management and other employees solve problems during the improvement journey. The author outlines the problem-solving steps such as selecting the issue, searching for data to describe the situation, analyzing the data/facts to obtain root causes of the performance gap, selecting a solution, conducting a pilot test, evaluating performance and standardizing, reflect and repeat the entire process

The method, according to the author, provides a record of the decision making process. William Bridges (1995) states that today's organizations are being transformed from a structure built out of job to s field out of work needing to be done. The author concludes that all these fall within the general category of principle and practices described by "Total Quality Management" (TQM), and "Total Quality Control" (TQC), and "Continuous Quality Improvement" (CQI). According to John MacDonald (1998) the concept of Total Quality Management was not totally new to evolutionary companies, since most had been focusing on quality goods and services. This point is exemplified by the approach of 3M and General Motors. Total Quality Management was profoundly influenced by developments in Japan, but it is not a phenomenon that can be bonded "Made in Japan." According to Dennis Waitley (1995) the new employee paradigms conforms to the concept of principles of Total Quality Management and are clearly stated as Autonomy and empowerment, meaningful work, career path, incentives, flexible schedule and team leadership.

In asserting the significance of TQM, Paul Neblock (1992) says that TQM is a structured program an organization uses to continually improve its operation; Management totally rethinks how the organization is run and restructures it for maximum effectiveness. Neblock further state that the cultural changes required by TQM empowers staff members so that they have more say on how decisions are made, thereby reducing turnover and fostering the teamwork that is a crucial element of a successful TQM program. Neblock, (1992) asserts that the heart of TQM is meeting the needs of customers who are both external and internal.

Collaboration is the premier candidate to replace hierarchy as the organizing principle for leading and managing the 21st century workplace, Edward E, Marshall (1995). He further reasserted the importance of this principle by outlining seven core values, which add up to its significance and continue to surface again and again as the basis for effective work relationships. Some of these values are respect for people, honor and integrity, ownership, alignment, consensus, full responsibility, trust-based relationships, and recognition and growth.

Edward E. Marshall further outlined some of the benefits of Collaboration such as faster decision-making, reduction in cycle time, increased productivity, and increased return on investment, increased span of control, more responsibility and accountability, reduction in conflict, higher quality and customer-driven decisions.

The icon of modern management, Peter F. Drucker (1998) expanded on the need for change into modern Organizational Management, a Total Quality Management style by justifying through seven underlying assumptions about organizations that are out of date which state that:

- There is only one right way to organize a business,
- The principles of management apply to business organizations,
- There is a single way to manage people,
- Technologies, markets and end users are fixed and rarely overlap,
- Management's scope is legally defined as applying only to an organization's assets and employees,
- Management's job is to run the business rather than to concentrate on what is happening outside the business.

In the healthcare industry quality improvement processes vary from one department to the next from one profession to the other. For example physicians might view a healthcare organization as a provider of processes for patient examination, patient testing, patient diagnosis and treatment. Healthcare administrators might view the activities in terms of admitting patients, tracking patient services, discharging patients and billing for the cost of services. Laboratory analysts might view their work as processes for acquiring samples, analyzing samples, performing quality control and releasing patient test results.

6:04- BASIC TOTAL QUALITY MANAGEMENT FRAMEWORK

The effective and efficient implementation of the Total Management strategy in an organization depends on some basic and fundamental activities and processes. These all help to define the quantity and quality of work and the various protocol and ethical standards required in the implementation process. Some of these activities are the Goals, Objectives and Philosophy, Quality Assessment, Quality Control, Quality Processes and Processing. The relationship among these processes is thus:

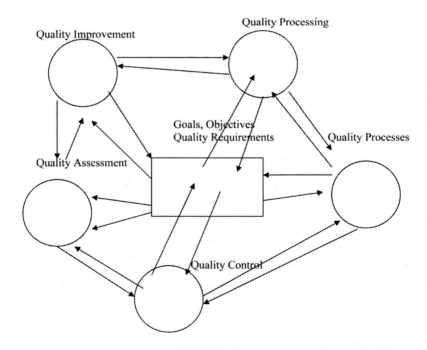

Total Quality Management is ineffective and inefficient without these processes and relationships.

6:05- BASIC TENETS OF TOTAL QUALITY MANAGEMENT

Total Quality Management has some basic tenets, which continue to influence its implementation across corporations such as: -

6:05:01- Systematic Approach to Problems:
Problems or opportunities for improvement are dealt with in many different ways, but quality organizations use a systematic, database approach to avoid mistakes and to eliminate short-term fixes that result in greater problems in the future - TQM is not a "quick fix."

6:05:02- Focus on Action:
Posters, T-shirts and other promotional items do not improve quality on their own. Without claims of quality, these promotional items become nothing more than great jobs. TQM is not conveyed by slogans, but through the actions of leaders and all employees.

6:05:03- Accepted and Practiced by All:
In order to work, TQM must be integrated into the daily operations of the entire organization. All must reach the philosophies of TQM because it is not a departmental or specialist function.

6:05:04- Change in Culture:
TQM involves many changes in individual thinking and organizational philosophy, and this does not happen overnight.

6:05:05- Commitment to Top Leadership:
Without commitment from the top, TQM simply will not work, because its success depends on good leadership. Leaders cannot delegate responsibility for Total Quality

6:05:06- Continuous, Systematic Improvement:
TQM affects the basic operational systems of an organization and provides for continuous improvement of these and all other day-to-day operations.

6:05:07- Long-Term Commitment:

TQM is infinite, a long-term project reading continuous efforts to improve systems and adjust to the changing demand of customers.

6:06- THE GURUS OF TOTAL QUALITY MANAGEMENT

Today, there are dozens of organizations practicing quality maintenance and improvement under different names and with varied approaches. There are, however, three pioneers of Total Quality Management on whose thesis and concepts we depend on today. They are W. Edwards Deming, Joseph M. Juran and Philip B. Crosby. Corporations such as AT&T, Chrysler, Dow Chemical, Ford, General Motors, IBM and Xerox originally based their quality systems on the philosophies delivered by these three innovators.

6:06: 01-W. EDWARDS DEMING'S 14 POINTS FOR QUALITY IMPROVEMENT

Deming is credited with much of Japan's industrial escalation and centralization after World War II. While working for the US State Department in the late 1940s, he was sent to Japan, where he taught his methods. Along with his 14 points, Deming's philosophy relies heavily on statistical process control. Deming believes that the majority of quality problems are caused by ineffective management practices. His 14 points for quality improvement are: -

1) Create and publish to all employees a statement of the aims and purposes of the company or other organization. The management must demonstrate constantly their commitment to this statement.
2) Learn the new philosophy, top management and everybody.
3) Understand the purpose of inspection, for improvement of processes and reduction of costs.
4) End the practice of awarding business on the basis of price tag alone.

5) Improve constantly and forever the system of production & service.
6) Institute training of Personnel.
7) Teach and institute leadership
8) Drive out fear. Create trust. Create a climate for innovation.
9) Optimize toward the aims and purposes of the company, the efforts of teams, groups and staff areas.
10) Eliminate exhortations for the workforce.
11) 11a. Eliminate numerical quotas for production instead learn and institute methods for improvement.
12) 11b. Eliminate Management By Objectives (M.B.O). Instead, learn the capabilities of processes, and how to improve them.
13) Remove barriers that rob people of pride of workmanship.
14) Encourage education and self-improvement for everyone.
15) Take action to accomplish the transformation.

6:06:02- JOSEPH M. JURAN'S 10 STEPS TO QUALITY IMPROVEMENT

Juran, like Deming, was instrumental in helping Japan rebuild its industrial base following World War II. His work is greatly concerned with eliminating production flows, and, he focuses more on improvements within the "parts" of Joseph M. Juran's 10 steps to Quality Improvement are as follows:

1) Build awareness of the need and opportunity for improvement.
2) Set goals for improvement.
3) Organize to reach the goals.
4) Provide training.
5) Carry out projects to solve problems.
6) Report progress.
7) Give recognition.
8) Community results.
9) Keep score.

10) Maintain momentum by making annual improvement part of the regular system and processes of the company.

6:06:03-PHILIP B. CROSBY'S 14 STEPS TO QUALITY IMPROVEMENT

Crosby believes that quality is measurable and is the responsibility of everyone in an organization. He is very "bottom-lining" oriented and believes that quality is the key to an organization's financial success. Philip B. Crosby's 14 steps to Quality Improvement are as follows:

1) Make it clear that leadership is committed to quality.
2) Form quality improvement teams with representatives from each department.
3) Determine where current and potential quality problems lie.
4) Evaluate the quality awareness and personal concern of all employees.
5) Raise the quality awareness and personal concerns of all employees.
6) Take actions to correct problems identified through previous steps.
7) Establish a committee for the zero defects program.
8) Train supervisors to actively carry out their part of the quality improvement program.
9) Hold a "zero defects day" to let all employees realize that there has been a change.
10) Encourage individuals to establish improvement goals for themselves and their groups.
11) Encourage employees to communicate to leadership the obstacles they face in attaining their improvement goals.
12) Recognize and appreciate those who participate.
13) Establish quality councils to community on a regular basis.
14) Do it all over again to emphasize that quality improvement never ends.

6:06:04- WALTER A. SHEWHART

Pioneer of modern Quality Control:\

- Recognized the need to separate variation into assignable and unassignable causes
- Founder of the control chart (e.g. X-Bar and R-chart)
- Originator of the plan-to-check-act cycle
- Successfully integrated statistics, engineering and economics
- Defined quality in terms of subjective quality (quality to how people perceive things, value), and objective quality (quality of a thing independent of people).

6:06:05- KAORU ISHIKAWA

Kaoru Ishikawa developed the concept of true and substitute quality characteristics:

- True characteristics are the customer's view
- Substitute characteristics are the producer's view
- The degree of match between true and substitute ultimately determines customer satisfaction
- -He also advocated for the 7 tools (e.g. cause-and-effect diagrams)
- -Advanced the use of quality circles (worker quality teams)
- - Developed the concept of Japanese Total Quality Control
  - Quality first- not short term profits
  - Next process is your customer
  - Use facts and data to make presentations
  - Respect for humanity as a management philosophy-full participation
  - Cross-functional management

6:06:06- SHIGEO SHINGO

*Advanced the replacement statistical process control with source inspection, i.e. controlling quality at the source through sampling inspection

* Set up poke-yoke devices (mistake-proven devices) such as sensors and monitors to identify defects at the point they occur

*Referred to his system as "zero defects" approach because Zero defect is the ultimate goal

6:07- TOTAL QUALITY M MANAGEMENT CULTURE

The transformation from traditional approaches to Total Quality Management begins with the acceptance of new paradigms. Not only do we improve but also we learn to prosper and thrive in an ever-changing environment. It is helpful to compare the differences between organizations that use traditional methods to those that have implemented Total Quality Management. Areas affected include organizational structure, communication, decision-making regarding products and services, quality, attitudes toward change and improvement and staff development.

In traditional organizations, administrators supervise departments and interactions are through dominantly vertical lines of authority. The managers and specialist staff establish the management environment. Within the system, individual's achievements are rewarded, often fostering competition and resentment among peers. With Total Quality Management, teams direct the work processes, and the management environment grows out of the team structures. All team members have ownership in success, and team-oriented behavior and innovations are valued and recognized. Interactions occur within the teams and through the team processes, not only within departments. Traditionally, decisions are often based on assumptions and gut-level feelings rather that collected data. These decisions are made at the top levels within departments by individual managers and specialists, who dictate improvements to products and services. Departments are isolated in product and service design. Also, the traditional organization decides what to offer customers based on assumptions about customer's needs and preferences and cost of providing or improving products and services often rise according to the availability of funds.

When Total Quality Management is implemented, the commitment to quality ensures that when more resources are available, more is done. The goal is always to offer products and services at a lower cost, focusing on customer satisfaction. The input of identified customers is sought to determine what they want in terms of products and service. Rather than single departments, cross-functional teams develop these products and services, with improvement plans determined by teams of managers, employees, vendors, customers and partner organization. Decisions regarding products and services are based on scientific approaches in Total Quality Management environment. Employees are encouraged to use their intuition to lead them to problems, but trained to verify the nature of problems with hard data. Prevention of problems is the major emphasis with TQM. All work must contribute to the value of the product or service. Work processes that result in waste and errors are not tolerated. Under traditional management, there are standard levels of tolerance for errors and waste. Problems are addressed through inspection and fixing them after they occur. Short-term planning, based primarily on budge cycles, predominates in tradition organizations. The status quo is favored, and work is done according to precedence and pr-existing routines.

By contrast, with Total Quality Management, long-term planning is prevalent and is linked to a continuous focus on the mission of the organization. Change and continuing improvement are desired; innovation and creativity are encouraged; prudent risk is rewarded. This commitment in continuing improvement is reflected in the attitude that training and education of employees represents a valuable investment of resources, and the organization seeks to develop internal quality experts. This differs from the traditional approach, where expertise on quality is sought on the outside and investments in training and education of staff are seen as undesirable and non-productive expenses. The necessary element of commitment is fostered by demonstrations of leadership and cultivation of those who can champion the ideas. The leaders ship the environment by establishing support systems, removing barriers to communication and processes, and reassessing reward and recognition systems. Resources are provided through training, through making time available and through empowerment of individuals.

Envisioning the mission before doing anything else is essential. The vision provides clarity and purpose. Part of the process of developing Total Quality Management is building awareness of the importance of having vision.

To build awareness, leaders often must provide training, using external consultants and demonstrate commitment by their actions. Then, roles, which are in alignment with the mission, evolve based on the consistency of purpose, long-term commitment and customer focus. The entire quality structure grows out of this.

Empowerment means giving authority and responsibility commensurate with skills and maturity to everyone. These empowered individuals can then focus on achieving the vision and focusing involves establishing customer-centered goals based on the mission. The goals must be realistic and have broad applicability. They must be communicated throughout the organization and be relevant to every individual. The goals must then be translated into practice, aligning improvement efforts to organizational objectives. Customers and suppliers, as well as employees, need to share the focus; they need to understand needs, communicate requirements and share experience. At this point, continually improving quality then becomes possible. The organization is able to define standards through the processes of documenting the current status, maintaining and updating existing standards, and measuring performance against these standards. Performance can be evaluated in terms of goals and customer needs.

6:08- TOTAL QUALITY MANAGEMENT AS A FOUNDATION

TQM is the foundation for productive activities in business which include:

- Meeting Customer Requirements
- Reducing Development Cycle Times
- Just in Time/Demand Flow Manufacturing

- Improvement Teams
- Reducing Product and Service Costs
- Improving Administrative System Training

6:09- TEN STEPS TO TOTAL QUALITY MANAGEMENT

Effective and efficient implementation of a TQM strategy requires a systematic procedure involving the following steps:

- Pursue New Strategic Thinking
- Know Your Customers
- Set True Customer Requirements
- Concentrate on Prevention, not Correction
- Reduce Chronic Wastes
- Pursue a Continuous Improvement Strategy
- Use Structured Methodology for Process Improvement
- Reduce Variation
- Use a Balanced Approach
- Apply to All Functions

6:10- HISTORY OF QUALITY PARADIGMS

1-Customer-craft quality paradigm:
- Design and build each product for a particular customer
- Producer knows the customer directly

2- Mass production and inspection quality paradigm:
- Focus on design and building products for mass consumption
- Push product on the customer
- Quality is maintained by inspection and detecting bad products

3- TQM or customer-driven quality paradigm:
- Potential customers determine what to design and build
- High quality obtained by focusing on preventing problems and continuously reducing variability in all organizational processes;

6:11- TOTAL QUALITY LEADERSHIP

Leadership is the ability of an individual to influence, motivate, and enable others to contribute towards the effectiveness and success of the organization. Leadership directly impacts the effectiveness of costs, revenue generation, services, satisfaction, earnings, market value, share price, social capital, engagement and sustainability.

Leadership scope range from youth activities to families, army, bands, tribes, states, nations, organizations and empires.

Leadership and management are two very complex concepts and Warren Bennis (1989) explains this dichotomy among them as follows:

- Managers administer, leaders innovate,
- Managers ask how and when, Leaders ask what and why,
- Managers focus on systems, Leaders focus on people,
- Managers do things right, Leaders do the right things,
- Managers maintain, Leaders develop,
- Managers rely on control, Leaders inspire trust,
- Managers have a short-term perspective, Leaders have a long-term perspective,
- Managers accept the status-quo, Leaders challenge the status-quo
- Managers have an eye on the bottom-line, Leaders have an eye on the horizon,
- Managers imitate, Leaders originate,
- Managers emulate the classic good soldier, Leaders have their own person,
- Mangers copy, Leaders show originality

Leadership Styles are vision, passion and self-sacrifice, confidence, determination and persistence, image-building, role-modeling, external representation, expectation and Confidence in followers, selective motivation, frame alignment and inspirational communication

Qualities of Good Leadership are, setting directions, empowering others, collaborative working, political astuteness, intellectual flexibility, delivering services, leading change through people, accountability, strategic planning, self-belief and confidence, drive for improvement, originality in thought and actions, personal integrity, optimism, results-oriented and initiative and entrepreneurial drive

CHAPTER SEVEN

7:00- OTHER SUSTAINABLE MANAGEMENT CONCEPTS

7:01- SIX SIGMA METHODOLOGY

The Six Sigma Methodology is a business-driven multi-faceted approach to process improvement, reduced cost and increased profitability with defects-free processes and products as its ultimate performance goal thereby giving room for project sustainability. It was developed by Motorola in the 1980's in response to the CEO's driven challenges to achieve a tenfold reduction in product failure in five years. The Six Sigma Methodology seeks to improve the quality of process outputs by identifying and removing the causes of defects and minimizing variability in manufacturing and business processes. It uses a set of quality management and statistical methods to create a special infrastructure of people within the organization such as Champions, Black Belts, Green Belts, and Yellow Belts who are experts in the implementation of these methods.

A Sigma process is one in which 99.99966% of the products manufactured are expected to have zero defects. The prime goal is improving customer satisfaction, profitability and elimination of defects and all based on the following statistical thinking paradigm:

- Everything is a process,
- All processes have inherent variability

- Data is used to understand the variability and drives process improvement decisions.

The Six Sigma doctrine advocates for continuous efforts to achieve stable and predictable process results; manufacturing and business processes that can be measured, analyzed, improved and controlled; and achieving sustained quality improvements requiring commitment from the entire organization.

Some major quality management tools used in the Six Sigma implementation are Variance Analysis, Business Process Mapping, Cause and Effects diagrams, Control Charts, Correlation Charts, Cost-Benefit Analysis, Cost-Effectiveness Analysis, Experimentation Design, Histograms, Pareto Charts, Regression Analysis, Root Cause analysis and Run Charts.

Effective and efficient implementation through the Six Sigma Methodologies requires the assignment of roles and responsibilities to organizational staffs involved in the process. Some major roles in the process are:

- Executive Leadership- this includes the CEO, President and other top management members of the organization responsible for setting the vision for Six Sigma implementation.
- Champions- they are drawn from upper management and they are responsible for across the board and integrated approach in information dissemination for implementation
- Master Black Belts- they are identified by champions as coaches and ensure consistency in application across various functions and departments
- Green Belts are the employees who implement the Six Sigma in compliance with the standards set.

Methodologies:

DMAIC: Define, Measure, Analyze, Improve, Control

Define: To define the process improvement goals that are consistent with customer demands and enterprise strategy. The tools are Benchmark, Baseline, Contract Charter, and Voice of the Customer, Quality Function department, Process Flow Map, Project Management, Management by Fact.

Measure: This is the measurement of the current process and collection of relevant data for future comparison. Tools are Defect Metrics, Data Collection, Forms, Plans and logistics, Sampling Techniques

Analyze: This is verification of relationship and casualty of factors. Tools are Cause and Effects Diagrams, Failure Modes and Effects Analysis, Decision and Risk Analysis, Statistical Inferences, Control Charts, Capability, Reliability Analysis, Root Cause Analysis

Improve: This is to optimize the process based upon the analysis using techniques like design and experiments. Tools are Design of Experiments, Modeling, and Robust design

Control: This is to ensure that any variances are corrected before they result in defects. Tools are Statistical Controls, Control Charts, Time series Methods, Non-Statistical Controls, Procedural Adherence, Performance Management, and preventive Activities.

DMADV: Define, Measure, Analyze, Design, Verify

Other Six Sigma methodologies:
CDOC- Conceptualize, Design, Optimize, Control
DCCDI- Define, Customer Concept, Design, Implement
DCDOV- Define, Concept, Design, Optimize, Verify

DIDOVM- Define, Identify, Design, Optimize, Verify, Monitor
DMADO- Define, Measure, Analyze, Design, Optimize, Verify
DMAIIC- Define, Measure, Analyze, Improve, Implement, Control
DMEDI- Define, Measure, Explore, Develop, Implement
IDOV- Identify, Design, Optimize, Validate
IIDOV- Invent, Innovate, Develop, Optimize, Validate
MMEEDDIICC- Map & Measure, Explore & Evaluate, Define & Describe, Implement & Improve, Control & Confirm
VCPCIA- Visualize, Commit, Prioritize, Characterize, Improve, Achieve

All these facilitate the effective and efficient identification, conceptualization, feasibility studies, design, analysis, monitoring and evaluation of projects. They all set standards for project implementation, measurement of inputs and outputs thus giving room for their sustainability in the marketplace.

7:03- TQM AND THE INTERNATIONAL ORGANIZATION FOR STANDARDIZATION (ISO) SERIES STANDARDS

The International Organization for Standardization (ISO) standardizes, organizes and controls operations in the manufacturing and service industries. It provides for consistent dissemination of information, improves various aspects of the business-based use of statistical data and analysis, acceptance of the system as a standard for ensuring quality in a global market, enhancing customer responsiveness to products and services and encouraging improvement. The standards are useful to industrial and business organizations of all types, to governmental and other regulatory bodies, to trade officials, to conformity assessment officials, to suppliers and customers of products and services in public and private sectors, and to people in general as consumers and end users.

The ISO Quality Standard sets in place a system to depend on a strategy whose implementation is the basis for a Total Quality Management system. The standards contribute to making the development, manufacturing and supply of products and services more efficient, safer and cleaner and trade between countries easier and fairer, which is the fundamental philosophy of the Total Quality Management concept. They provide the basis for health, safety and environmental legislation as well as technology transfer.

The ISO 8000-2000 family of Standards was developed to assist organizations and sizes, to implement and operate an effective and efficient quality management system made of four core standards: -

A   9001 Model for quality assurance in design, development, production, installation and servicing,
B)   9002 Model for quality assurance in production, installation and servicing,
C)   9003 Model for quality assurance in final inspection and test,
D)   9004 Model Guidelines for development of quality system elements and management.

The ISO 9000 series provides the company with a quality system that: -

1)   Standardizes, organizes and controls operations,
2)   Provides for consistent dissemination of information,
3)   Improves various aspects of the business- based use of statistical data and analysis,
4)   Acceptance of the system as a standard for ensuring quality in a global market,
5)   Enhances customer responsiveness to products and service,
6)   Encourages improvement.

The ISO 9000 series standards are organized according to functions, such as: document and data control, and contract review therefore they are set forth in a logical format. Organized in outline form they provide a template for each function that affects the quality of the product or service in the company. Guidelines provided by the standards establish a consistent approach to policy documentation. Controls are set forth in the standards in the areas of document control of non-conforming product. Three areas of the standards, in particular, provide for consistent dissemination of information: -

❖ Control of quality records insures that pertinent records are maintained regarding quality records,

❖ Design control eliminates ad-hoc engineering changes that are not communicated with all parties involved in the process,

❖ Document and data control standards require a system of document revision, document distribution, removal of obsolete documents, and document approval.

The ISO 9000 series standards require the company to identify the need for statistical techniques and to implement and control such techniques. The standards specifically point to process capability and product characteristics. The standards allow the company the flexibility to use those statistical techniques that would be appropriate for their industry. Additionally, the standards refer to the use of both corrective and preventative action, and effective internal auditing. These techniques and systems improve business processes by using database management rather than instinct and hunches.

7:04- CONFIGURATION MANAGEMENT

Configuration Management is the process of managing products, facilities and processes by managing the information about them, including changes, and ensuring that they are what they are supposed to be in the case.

Configuration Management is most applied in engineering and computer generated products such as hardware, software, firmware, middleware, user interaction and documentation. It provides visibility and control of performance, functional and physical attributes

Scope:

- Defining the configuration management roles and responsibilities at the organizational level
- Orderly establishment, documentation and maintenance of product performance, function and physical attributes.
- Management of changes to the attributes
- Access to accurate information essential to the product's development, procurement, production, use, maintenance and eventual retirement.

Benefits:

- Improve capability
- Improve performance, reliability or maintainability
- Extend life of product
- Reduce cost
- Reduce risk and liability
- Correct defects

7:05- HUMAN RESOURCE MANAGEMENT

Human Resource Management is the strategic and meticulous approach to the management of an organization's most valued assets-the people working there, who individually or collectively contribute to the achievement of the organization's objective. Some processes performed by the human resource department to achieve its goals and objectives are workforce planning, recruitment, induction and orientation, skills management, training and development, personnel administration, compensation in wage and salary, time management, travel management, payroll, employee benefits administration, personnel cost planning and performance appraisal.

Personnel functions help to shape TQM activities through reviewing current organizational cultures or designing managerial development courses for employees. TQM therefore can only achieve its objective with contributions from the Human Resource Department. Moreover, for TQM to be implemented in an organization, the Human Resource Department must approve of it and define the vision statement and goal. TQM has clear implications for human resources in terms of employees taking greater responsibility for quality, having accountability for its achievements, or in terms of the introduction of team working principles into organizations. TQM is consistent with human resource management on employee compliance, commitment and it identifies line managers as key players in the managing of people in an organization. Both TQM and Human Resource management call for the involvement of top management as a strategic approach in the management of human resources.

5:05:01-The main features of Human Resource Management are Personnel administration, Personnel management, Manpower management and Industrial management

5:05:02- Major Components of Human Resources management

A) Employee Recruitment and Development which involves workforce planning, job development, responsibilities and roles, recruitment, outsourcing, screening applicants and hiring new employees
B) Providing benefits and compensation to employees
C) Employee orientation/Training which involves, career development, employee orientation, leadership development, management development, personal development, supervisor development and training and development
D) Compliance and Regulation which comprises personnel policies and records, employee laws, topics and issues and ethics
E) Safe Work Environment which involves diversity management, drugs issues, employee assistance program, medical issues at the workplace, personal wellness and safety in the workplace
F) Sustaining Employees in the Workplace and this involves employee performance management, group performance management, interpersonal skills, personal productivity and retaining employees.

7:06- CAPACITY BUILDING

Capacity Building is the creation of an enabling environment with appropriate policy and legal framework, institutional development, including community participation, human resources development and strengthening of management systems. This is a long-term continuing process in which all stakeholders participate in various capacities. Capacity Building is the process of developing and strengthening the skills, instincts, abilities, processes and resources that organizations and communities need to survive, adapt, and thrive in a fast-changing world such as health, education, agriculture, transportation etc. Capacity Building may also be identified as activities that strengthen the knowledge, skills, abilities and behaviors of individuals and improve institutional structures such that the organization can efficiently meets its mission, goals, values, philosophy and objectives in a more sustainable way. This encompasses developing the country's human, scientific, technological, organizational, institutional, and resource capabilities.

The fundamental goal of capacity building is to enhance the ability to evaluate and address the crucial questions related to policy choices and modes of implementation among development options.

Some agencies providing capacity building in developing countries are the World Bank, International Monetary Fund, United Nations Development Program, Food and Agricultural organization, NGO's, Asian Development Bank and the Population Council.

For most organizations, capacity building relates to improved governance, leadership, mission and strategy, administration, human resources, financial management, legal issues, program development, implementation and management, fundraising and income generation, diversity partnerships and collaboration, advocacy, marketing, planning, monitoring etc. One important mechanism for capacity building is partnership development which gives local NGO's access to knowledge and skills and funding opportunities, replicable models for addressing community needs and managing resources, strategies for advocacy, government relations and public outreach.

7:06:01- Areas of Capacity Building:

o Hunan Resource Development
o Organizational Development
o Institutional and legal framework development

7:06:02- Capacity Building Agents

o Management Consultants- they provide expertise, coaching, training and referrals.

o Researchers- They identify issues and trends and build knowledge for nonprofits

o Management Support Organizations- These are nonprofit consulting firms that provide consultation, training, resources, research, referrals and other services to NGO's

o Grant makers- They offer grants for training and consultancy

o Universities/Academic Centers- They provides formal training and certification opportunities. They also conduct research and have resource centers.

o Intermediate and Umbrella Organizations- These are attorneys, accountants, technology firms, national and international organizations, coalitions, think thanks and research institutions.

7:07- KNOWLEDGE MANAGEMENT

Knowledge Management is a contemporary business discipline dealing gathering, organizing, sharing, and analyzing knowledge in terms of resources, documents and people's skills. It is involves the identification, creation, representation and distribution of knowledge.

Knowledge Management programs are tied to organizational objectives such as improved performance, competitive advantage, innovation, developmental processes and general development of collaborative practices. Knowledge Management is synonymous to continuous improvement, lifelong learning and learning organizations.

7:07:01- Some Knowledge Management Programs:

- Managing intellectual capital and intellectual assets in the workforce such as expertise and know-how possessed by employees
- Managing the proliferation of data and information in complex business environments
- Increasing network connectivity between employees and external groups to improve information exchange
- Leveraging the expertise of people across the board
- Facilitating and managing organizational innovation and learning
- Making available increased knowledge content in the development and provision of products and services.

7:07:02- Processes in Knowledge Management

Gathering- Data entry, OCR and scanning, voice input, pulling information from various

Organizing- Cataloging, Indexing, Filtering, Linking

Refining- Contextualizing, Collaborating, Compacting, Projecting, Mining

Dissemination- Flow, Sharing, Alert, Push

Asset Utilization

Knowledge Evaluation

Knowledge Improvement

Knowledge Accumulation

Knowledge generation

Knowledge Protection

7:07:03- Disciplines and Technologies of Knowledge Management

○ Cognitive Science- Insights from how we learn and know improves tools and techniques for gathering and transferring knowledge

○ Groupware (Computer-supported Collaborative Work)- Sharing and collaborating is vital for organizational knowledge management through intranet etc

○ Library and Information Science- Catalogues, references, dictionaries all classify knowledge for research

○ Document Management- This helps in content accessibility and reusability

○ Decision Support Systems- Insights from cognitive sciences, management sciences, computer sciences, operational research helps to produce computerized artifacts for quantitative and qualitative analysis and these are decision tools for managers and organizations.

○ Relational and Object Database- This is used for managing structured data and it helps in representing and managing knowledge resources.

○ Organizational Science- This is the science of managing organizational dealings with the need to manage knowledge.

7:08- SWOT ANALYSIS

SWOT is acronym for Strengths, Weaknesses, Opportunities and Threats. The SWOT analysis is a strategic planning tool used in the evaluation of most business operations nowadays. It is used in projects, programs, processes, activities, business ventures and organizations as a whole. Some examples for SWOT assessments are company position in the market, commercial viability, and method of sales distribution, a product or brand, a business idea, entering a new market or launching a new product, making an acquisition, partnership agreement, changing a supplier, outsourcing a service, activity or resource and an investment opportunity. It involves specifying the objectives, identifying the internal and external factors that are either favorable or unfavorable towards the realization of the objectives.

SWOT Analysis is used in decision-making, pre-crisis planning, and preventive crisis management. In corporate planning SWOT is used to set objectives, undertake environmental scanning, analysis of existing strategies, developing new strategies, establishing critical success factors, preparing operational and resource plans, and monitoring and evaluating results. SWOT is an auditing tool for the organization.

SWOT Analysis was the result of a research project by Albert S. Humphrey of Stanford Research Institute from 1960-1970 on the failure of organizations. Key findings in the research lead to the conclusion that in corporations, the Chief Executive should be the chief planner and his functional director's members of the planning team. In SWOT issues are sorted into program planning categories such as:

- Product- what is being sold
- Process- how it has been sold
- Customer- who is buying
- Distribution- how will products and services reach the customer
- Finance- cost, price and investments
- Administration- how to manage.

7:08:01- MAJOR CONSIDERATIONS IN SWOT

- Changes in competitive environments
- Changes in socio-cultural environments
- Changes in political environments

- Changes in legal environments
- Changes in internal organizational environments

7:08-02- EXAMPLES OF SWOT ACTIVITIES

7:08:02:01- STRENGTHS:

- Developed techniques
- Reputation in the market place
- Competitive advantages
- Resources, assets, people
- Experience, knowledge, data
- Financial reserves
- Marketing- reach, awareness, distribution
- Innovation
- Strategic location
- Price, value, quality
- Accreditation, qualifications, certifications
- Process, systems, IT Communication
- Management success
- Right product, quality and reliability

7:08:02:02- WEAKNESSES

- Shortage of consultants
- Gaps in capabilities
- Lack of competitive strength
- Poor reputation
- Financial problems
- Unmet deadlines
- Cash flow problems
- Unreliability and unpredictability of data
- Poor leadership
- Non accreditation

- No direct marketing experience
- No pilot or trial done
- No plans

7:08:02:03- OPPORTUNITIES

- Market developments
- Competitors vulnerabilities
- Industry or lifestyle trends
- Technological developments and innovations
- Global influences
- New markets-vertical or horizontal
- Niche target markets
- Business and product development
- Information and research
- Partnerships, agencies and distributions
- Volumes, production and economies
- Local competitors with poor products
- Good profit margins
- New specialist applications

7:08:02:04- THREATS

- Political effects
- Legislative effects
- Environmental effects
- IT developments
- Market demand
- New technologies
- Vital contracts and partners
- Loss of key staffs

SWOT is an assessment tool used to assess a company's viability and sustainability in the marketplace.

7:09- MONITORING AND EVALUATION

Monitoring is the systematic supervision of activities in progress to ensure that they are on curse and schedule in meeting objectives and performance targets. It is a test or sampling on a regular or ongoing basis of a system, program, project or activity for any changes in application performance, transaction, problems and potentials for changes as well as the effectiveness and efficiency. This involves a systematic collection and analysis of data as a project progresses. Generally, monitoring involves:

- Establishing indicators of efficiency, effectiveness and impact
- Setting up systems to collect information related to these indicators
- Collecting and recording the information
- Analyzing the information
- Using the information to inform day-to-day management

Evaluation is the systematic determination of the merits, worth and significance of something or following some certain set standards, an assessment of the degree to which a program, project, system or activity fulfils stated objectives and goals. This requires a comparison of actual project impact against the agreed strategic plans. Generally, evaluation involves:

- Looking at what the project or organization intended to achieve
- Assessing its progress towards what it was made to achieve
- Looking at the strategy of the project or organization
- Looking at how it worked

The bottom-line is that both monitoring and evaluation all focus on efficiency, effectiveness and impact of projects, programs or activities and through the two processes, we review progress, identify problems and potentials in planning and implementation, suggest possible solutions, raise questions, stimulate some reflection on the goals and objectives, provide information on insight and make necessary adjustments for improvement.

7:09:01- Objectives of Program Evaluation

- To inform decision on operations, policy, or strategy related to ongoing or future program interventions
- To promote accountability and transparency to stakeholders, decision-makers and donors
- To enable corporate learning and contribute to the body of knowledge on what works and what does not work and why
- To verify and improve program quality and management
- To identify successful strategies for extension, expansion and replication
- To modify unsuccessful strategies
- To measure the effects and benefits of programs and project intervention
- To give stakeholders the opportunity to have a say in program output and quality
- To justify and validate programs to donors, partners and constituencies
- To enhance the generation and use of value-added evaluative information

The American Evaluation Association (AEA) has some specific Guiding Principles established for various evaluation exercises such as Systematic Inquiry, Competence, Integrity and Honesty, Respect for People and Responsibilities for the General and Public Welfare.

1- Systematic Inquiry- Evaluators conduct systematic data-based inquiries
2- Competence- Evaluators provide competent performance to stakeholders
3- Integrity and Honesty- Evaluators display honesty and integrity in their own behavior and attempt to ensure the honesty and integrity of the entire evaluation process

4- Respect for People- Evaluators respect the security, dignity and self-worth of respondents, program participants, clients and other evaluation stakeholders

5- Responsibilities for the General and Public Welfare-Evaluators articulate and take into account the diversity of general and public interests and values that may be related to the evaluation.

7:09:02- Characteristics of Monitoring and Evaluation

Monitoring	Evaluation
Continuous	Periodic: at important milestones such as mid-term program implementation; at the end of program such as final report
Keeps track: oversight, analyses and document progress	In-depth Analysis; Compares planned with actual achievements
Focuses on inputs, activities, outputs, implementation processes, continued relevance, likely results at outcome level	Focuses on outputs in relation to inputs; results in relation to costs; processes used to achieve results; overall relevance; impact and sustainability
Answers what activities were implemented and results achieved	Answers why and how results were achieved. Contributes to building theories and models for change
Alerts managers to problems and provides options for corrective action	Provides managers with strategy and policy options
Self-assessment by program managers, supervisors, community stakeholders and donors	Internal and external analysis by program managers, supervisors, community stakeholders, donors, and external evaluators

Source: UNICEF, 1991

7:09:03- Types of Evaluations

1- Formative Evaluation

Formative Evaluation is exercised when new programs, new interventions, new procedures or new elements of existing programs are proposed. It is often during the pre-implementation or design phase of the project and emphasize needs assessment

2- Process Evaluation

Process Evaluation involves documenting actual program functioning and identifying barriers to implementation. This has to do more with program monitoring. This includes the identification of target population, description of services delivered, the use of resources and the qualifications and experiences of personnel working in them.

3- Outcome Evaluation

Outcome Evaluations are carried out to measure the effectiveness of a program and as such deal with program output or results. Criteria used are objectivity, measurability, attributable and sensitivity.

4- Cost-Effectiveness Analysis

This evaluates the cost of the program against its effectiveness and efficiency in terms of targeted population or client served, services rendered and cost etc

5- Cost-Benefit Analysis

This evaluation examines the financial, economic, social, moral, psychological and other costs of the program against its economic, financial, social, moral, psychological and other benefits.

7:09:04- Indicators of Monitoring and Evaluation

7:09:04-A-Economic Development Indicators

- ❏ Average annual household income
- ❏ Average weekly/monthly wages
- ❏ Employment, by age group
- ❏ Unemployment, by age group, by gender
- ❏ Employment, by occupation, by gender
- ❏ Government employment
- ❏ Earned income levels
- ❏ Average length of unemployment period
- ❏ Default rates on loans
- ❏ Ratio of home owners to renters
- ❏ Per capita income
- ❏ Average annual family income
- ❏ % people below the poverty line
- ❏ Ratio of seasonal to permanent employment
- ❏ Growth rate of small businesses

7:09:04-B- Social Development Indicators

- ❏ Death rate
- ❏ Life expectancy at birth
- ❏ Infant mortality rates
- ❏ Causes of death
- ❏ Number of doctors per capita
- ❏ Number of hospital beds per capita
- ❏ Number of nurses per capita
- ❏ Literacy rates, by age and gender
- ❏ Student: teacher ratios
- ❏ Retention rate by school level
- ❏ School completion rates by exit points
- ❏ Public spending per studnet

- Number of suicides
- Causes of accidents
- Dwellings with running water
- Dwellings with electricity
- Number of homeless
- Number of violent crimes
- Birth rate
- Fertility rate
- Gini distribution of income (see Glossary of Terms)
- Infant mortality rate
- Rates of hospitalisation
- Rates of HIV infection
- Rates of AIDS deaths
- Number of movie theatres/swimming pools per 1000 residents
- Number of radios/televisions per capita
- Availability of books in traditional languages
- Traditional languages taught in schools
- Time spent on listening to radio/watching television by gender
- Number of programmes on television and radio in traditional languages and/or dealing with traditional customs
- Church participation, by age and gender

7:09:04-C- Political/Organisational Development Indicators

- Number of community organisations
- Types of organised sport
- Number of tournaments and games
- Participation levels in organised sport
- Number of youth groups
- Participation in youth groups
- Participation in women's groups
- Participation in groups for the elderly
- Number of groups for the elderly
- Structure of political leadership, by age and gender

- Participation rate in elections, by age and gender
- Number of public meetings held
- Particiaption in public meetings, by age and gender

7:09:05- Difference Between Monitoring and Evaluation

CRITERIA	MONITORING	EVALUATION
Objective	To track changes from baseline conditions to desired outcomes	To validate what results were achieved and how and why they were or not achieved
Focus	Focuses on output of projects and programs	Compares planned with intended outcomes achieved. Focuses on how and why outputs and strategies contributed to achievement of outcomes. Focuses on question of relevance, effecitvieness, sustainability and chamge
Methodology	Tracks and assesses performsnce through analysis and comparison of indicators over time	Evaluates achievement of outcomes by comparing before and after the interventions. Relies on monitoring data to information from external sources.
Conduct	Continuous and systematic by Task Managers, Project Managers, Program Managers and key partners.	Time-bound, periodic, in-depth. External evaluators and partners
Use	Alerts manager to problems in performance, provide options for corrective actions and helps demonstrate accountability	Provides managers with strategy and policy options, provides basis for learning and demonstrates accountability.

Source: UNDP Handbook on Monitoring and Evaluation for Results.

7:09:06- Designing the Monitoring and Evaluatiojn Process

Monitoring and Evaluation designs may vary depending on the type of information to be collected, the purpose of the evaluation, the nature of the project and the budget available. They can be Quantitative, Qualitative, Experimantal, Quasi-Experimental ard Descriptive designs.

Quantitative designs methods explain 'what', 'how much', or 'how many'. These deal often with numbers.

Qualitative designs answer 'why' and 'how' questions. When evaluating innovative projects and programs such as technology applications, qualitative designs are more appropriate

Experimental and Quasi-Experimental designs try to estimate the effects and impact of projects and programs

Descriptive designs try to describe what happened in terms of activities, outputs and performance.

CHAPTER EIGHT

8:00- SUSTAINABLE PROJECT MANAGEMENT PROCESSES

The main project management processes are planning, directing, controlling and administration.

8:00:01-PLANNING: This involves:

- Defining project objectives
- Listing tasks
- Estimating effort and duration
- Determining task interdependence
- Scheduling tasks
- Budgeting project expenditures
- Scheduling project resources
- Balancing project resources
- Obtaining project plan approval

8:00:02- DIRECTING: This involves:

- Reviewing plan objectives with project team
- Assigning tasks to project members
- Reviewing criteria for task completion
- Motivating project team

8:00:03- CONTROLLING: This involves:

- Reviewing project progress
- Controlling project changes
- Reporting project progress
- Re-planning of project activities
- Conducting project reviews
- Reviewing and approving completed work
- Assuring delivery of project products
- Resolving project issues
- Closing the project

8:00:04- ADMINSTRATION: This involves:

- Recruiting the project team
- Developing project personnel
- Developing and maintaining policies, standards, guidelines and procedures
- Authorizing project expenditures

8:01- THE PROJECT PLAN PROCESS

PROJECT PLAN:

8:01-01- PREPARATION:

- Perform feasibility study
- Perform risk and impact assessment
- Document business case
- Document umbrella contract
- Obtain interim funding

8:01-02- PROJECT DEFINITION:

- Define Project
- Document project definition report
- Document project plan
- Document quality plan
- Document resource terms of reference
- Document vendor/client contract

8:01-03- PROJECT ANALYSIS:

- Document business requirements
- Document technology requirements

8:01-04- PROJECT DESIGN:

- Document current/future state design
- Define process model
- Define organizational chart
- Define location chart
- Define data/application architecture
- Define organizational change strategy
- Define development strategy
- Define testing strategy
- Define operational support strategy

8:01-05- PROJECT DEVELOPMENT:

- Build IT infrastructure
- Build prototype
- Design physical prototype
- Build physical prototype
- Test physical prototype
- Implement prototype

- Market and approve prototype
- Develop database
- Produce database design
- Build database
- Build database testing routine
- Perform database unit testing
- Develop data migration
- Produce data migration design
- Build application software
- Design software configuration
- Install and configure software components
- Build software testing routines
- Build business infrastructure
- Build business processes
- Document detailed process model
- Document detailed procedures
- Unit test of processes and procedures
- Undertake communications
- Document communication plan
- Communicate organizational changes
- Communicate system changes
- Measure communication effectiveness
- Undertake training
- Document training procedure and handbook
- Perform organizational training and re-skilling
- Measure training effectiveness
- Build physical location
- Produce physical location design
- Purchase/build location
- Unit testing of location

8:01-06- TESTING

- Build test packs and scripts
- Perform system testing
- Perform integration testing
- Perform user acceptance testing
- Review implementation readiness
- Authorize implementation

8:01-07- PROJECT IMPLEMENTATION:

- Schedule implementation
- Implement IT infrastructure
- Implement data migration
- Check data validity
- Implement application software
- Test installed application software
- Implement business infrastructure
- Implement processes
- Distribute process/procedural documentation
- Implement organizational changes

8:01-08- ACCEPTANCE:

- Perform full user acceptance
- Perform final operational acceptance
- Signoff implementation completion

8:01-09- REVIEW:

- Document post implementation review

8:01-10- PROJECT CLOSE DOWN

- Document project closedown report
- Release resources
- Perform contract closeout/change-over

8:01-11- OPERATIONAL SUPPORT

- Manage operational schedule
- Manage availability
- Manage capacity
- Manage performance
- Manage back-up and recovery
- Manage disaster recovery
- Manage Security
- Manage data
- Manage on-going training

8:02- FEASIBILITY STUDY PROCESS

8:02:01- Executive Summary

8:02:02- Background

8:02:03- Current Business Review
8:02:03:01- Current Business Processes
8:02:03:02- Current Business Organizations
8:02:03:03- Current Business Locations
8:02:03:04- Current Business Data
8:02:03-05- Current Business Application
8:02:06- Current Business Technologies

8:02-04- Current Business problems

8:2:04:01- Business Process Problems

8:2:04:02- Business Organization Problems

8:2:04:03- Business Location Problems

8:2:04:04- Business Data Problems

8:2:04:05- Business Application Problems

8:2:04:06- Business Technologies problems

8:2:05- Business Requirements

8:2:05:01- Business Process requirements

8:2:05:02- Business Organizational Requirements

8:2:05:03- Business Location requirements

8:2:05:04- Business Data Requirements

8:2:05:05- Business Application Requirements

8:2:05:06- Business Technology Requirements

8:2:05:07- Other Business Requirements

8:2:06- Business Options

8:2:06:01- Options Identification

8:2:06:02- Options Analysis

8:206:03- Options Selection

8:2:07- Recommendations

8:03- QUALITY PLAN PROCESS

8:3:01- Project Definition

8:3:01:01- Background

8:3:01:02- Project Vision

8:3:01:03- Project Objectives

8:3:01:04- Project Scope

8:3:01:05- Project Deliverables

8:3:02- Project Quality Policy
8:3:02:01- Quality Statement

8:3:02:02- Quality Targets

:

8:3:03- Project Organization
8:3:03:01- project Resources

8:3:03:02- Project Roles and Responsibilities

8:3:03:03- Project review group

8:3:03:04- Project Manager

8:3:03:05- Project Team member

8:3:03:06- Project Milestones

8:304- Project Processes
8:3:04-01- Methodology

8:3:04:02- Change Management Process

8:3:04:03- Configuration Management Process

8:3:04:04- Issue Management Process

8:3:04:05- Defect Management Process

8:3:04:06- Problem Management Process

8:3:04:07- Risk Management Process

8:3:04:08- Quality Management Process

8:3:04:09- Document Management Process

8:3:04:10- Acceptance Management Process

8:3:04:11- Payment Management Process

8:3:04:12- Timesheet Management Process

8:3:04:13- Reporting Process

8:04- CHANGE MANAGEENT PROCESS

8:4:01- Overview
8:4:01:02- Change Process

8:4:01:03- Submit Change Request

8:4:01:04- Review Change Request

8:4:01:05- Identify Change Feasibility

8:4:01:06- Approve Change Request

8:4:01:07- Implement Change Request

8:4:02- Change Roles

8:4:02:01- Change Requestor

8:4:02:02- Change Managers

8:4:02:03- Change Feasibility Group

8:4:02:04- Change Approval Group

8:02:05- Change Implementation Group

8:4:03- Change Register

8:05- RISK MANAGEMENT PROCESS

8:5:01- Overview

8:5:02- Risk Processes

8:5:02:01- Summary

8:5:02:02- Raise Risk

8:5:02:03- Register Risk

8:5:02:04- Assign Risk

8:5:02:05- Implement Risk

8:5:03- Risk Roles

8:5:03:01- Risk Originator

8:5:03:02- Project Manager

8:5:03:03- Project Review group

8:5:03:04- Project Team

8:5:04- Risk Register

8:06- THE BUSINESS PLAN

8:6:01- Executive Summary

8:6:02- Introduction to the Business Plan

8:6:02: A- Cover Letter

8:6:02-B- Cover Sheet

8:6:02: C- Table of Contents

8:6:03- Business Identification

8:6:03: A- Name of the business

8:6:03: B- Business physical and P.O. address and email address

8:6:03-C-Business physical location

8:6:03-D- Business telephone, fax numbers

8:6:03-E- Business Tax identification number

8:6:03-F- Principals involved in the business and contact information

8:6:03-G- Business Accountant and contact information

8:6:03-H- Business Attorney and contact information

8:6:03-I- Business Bankers and contact information

8:6:03-J- Business Insurance Agent and contact information

8:6:04- Purpose of the Business

8:6:04: A- the goals of the proposed business

8:6:04: B- Business Acquisition or expansion

8:6:04: C- Management of the business

8:6:04: D- Finances needed for the business

8:6:04: G- Available collateral and market value

8:6:05- Description of the Business

8:6:05: A- Legal description of the proposed business

8:6:05: B- Place of business incorporation

8:06:05: C- Project date of operation

8:6:05: D- Operating schedule

8:6:05: E- Suppliers and subcontractors for the business

8:6:05: F- Market research carried out

8:6:05: G- Business competition

8:6:05: H- Project success for the business

8:6:06- The Market

8:6:06: A- Primary market-racial, age, sex, social, educational composition etc

8:6:06: B- Anticipated growth potential of the market

8:6:06: C- Pricing of products and services

8:6:06: D- Market competition

8:6:06: E- Business advertisement and promotion- logos, slogans, aids etc

8:6:07- Business Competition

8:6:07: A- Name of business nearest competitors

8:6:07: B- Competition strategy

8:6:07: C- Estimated market share and plans

8:6:08- Managing the Business

8:6:08: A- Curriculum Vitae of principals of the business

8:6:08: B- Job descriptions of each principal of the business

8:6:08: C- Salaries and fringe benefits

8:6:08: D- Consultants and other personnel outsourcing issues

8: 09- Business Personnel

8:6:09: A- Recruitment and hiring

8:6:09: A- Training and benefits to be provided

8:6:09: C- Succession policy in the business

8:6:10- Business Location

8:6:10: A- Reasons for choosing the business location

8:6:10: B- Business neighborhood

8:6:10: C- Zoning restrictions in the area

8:6:10: D- other locations exploited

8:6:10: E- Cost of rental or purchase

8:6:10: F- Leasing terms, taxes

8:6:10: G- Floor plan of the facility

8:6:11- Financial Information

8:6:11: A- Capital Requirements

8:6:11: B- Depreciable Assets

8:6:11: C- Balance Sheet

8:6:11: D- Break-Even Analysis

8:6:11: E- Project Income Statement

8:6:11: F- Cash Flow Projection and Analysis

8:6:12- Business Record Keeping

8:6:13- Business Miscellaneous Checklist

8:6:13: A- Status of business-franchise, LLC, INC etc

8:6:13: B- Copies of pertinent contracts

8:6:13: C- Copies of business agreements

8"6:13: D- Management contract

8:: 13: E- Maintenance agreements

8:13: F- Roster of customers, annual purchases, and terms

8:7:3: G- Principal Suppliers, annual volumes, and terms

8:6:13: H- Annual Report

8:6:13: I- Insurance carrier

8:6:13: J- Patents or copyrights

8:07- THE MARKETING PLAN

8:7:01- Cover Sheet- name address, contact information of stakeholders

8:7:02- Executive Summary- who, what, how, when, why

8:7:03- Industry Situational Analysis

8:7:03: A- SWOT Analysis-Strengths, Weaknesses, Opportunities, and Threats

8:7:03: B- PEST Analysis- Political/legal, Economic, Socio-cultural, Technological

87:04- Product/Services and Target Markets

8:7:04: A- Target market demographics

8:7:04: B- Industry or societal trends

8:7:04: C- Target customers' needs and wants

8:7:05- Marketing Strategy

8:7:06- Measurement Metrics

8:7:07- Forecasts and Financial Analysis

8:7:08- Conclusion

8:08- THE PROJECT PROPOSAL TEMPLATE

COVER PAGE

Project Title:	Name of Project
Sponsor:	XYZ Company
Reference Number:	000000000000
Project Duration:	Start Date and End Date
Total Amount Requested:	Itemized Breakdown of Cost
Contact Information:	Address, Phone, Email, Website
Validity of Proposal:	Days/Months/Years
Proposal Manager:	Sir Johnny MOR

Approved by _____ on _____

8:8-0- Executive Summary

A brief and focused description of the overall proposal, highlighting the theme, the company, the project team, their strengths, track record, the solution, deliverables, key advantages, possible potentials, problems and features that distinguish it from competitors.

8:8:01- Table of Contents

8:8:02- Glossary

8:8:03- BACKGROUND AND JUSTIFICATION

This section should provide a brief introduction to the current social and economic situation related to the geographic region and beneficiaries of the project. The background should also describe:

- the problem or critical issue which the proposal seeks to resolve
- how the proposal relates to other relevant national development strategies and policies
- whether there are other programmers and activities which will complement the proposal
- how the need for the project was determined
- how intended beneficiaries were involved in project identification and planning
- what kind of assistance the concerned governmental offices will provide
- what kind of resources the non-governmental community will provide

If a non-governmental organization has prepared the proposal, it is important to describe how concerned governmental officials were made aware of and/or were involved in project formulation.

Finally, the section should describe the relevant experience and capabilities of the project Implementing Agent, and the type and level of resources that the Implementing Agent will provide for project planning, implementation management and follow up.

8:8:04- OBJECTIVES

8:8:04-1- Development objective
the section should describe the way in project objectives are addressed in national development strategies and policies, in terms of specific programmers and how the proposed project will relate to these strategies and policies.

The discussion should indicate the specific national social and economic objectives to which the proposal, if successful, is expected to contribute, and how this is expected to contribute to improved well being and livelihood of the project beneficiaries and the larger community.

8:8:04-2- Immediate objectives
the immediate objectives section describes what the project is expected to achieve in terms of effects among intended beneficiaries. Specifically, the section discusses what changes are expected to occur among intended beneficiaries if project operations are successful. Changes can include new and improved technical skills and knowledge, increased income-generating capacities, and greater public awareness at the community, national, regional or international levels.

The section should also discuss whether project operations, if successful, will be extended to other locations as well as and whether the project experience can be applied to other sectors.

8:8:05- Summary of the Project

This section should provide a short description of the overall goals and objectives of the project and the main areas of concentration. It should be developed in a manner that can be used as a summary of the project.

It should also elaborate the linkages with the overall objectives of your organization.

8:8:06- Information about the organization

The Proposal should provide detailed information about the organization, beginning with full contact address and names of focal point for contacts.

Name of Organization:
Address:
Telephone:
Fax:
E-mail:

A description of the organization should also be provided in this section. This includes information on the objectives of the organization, structure and way of working, scope of programmed and previous experience relevant to the project area that the Expression of Interest relates to:
- Objectives of the organization
- Structure and way of working
- Scope of programmed in Mozambique
- Previous experience relevant to proposal contents

Contact person for the project in relation to this Expression of Interest
Name:
Position: _____

8:8:07- Project Plan

The project plan provides the substance of the proposed project and main elements of the Expression of Interest. It outlines the background to the project, overall objectives and planned activities. It is composed of the following areas:

8:8:07-1- The Project design and Proposal development

The process that has brought about the proposal and its submission

8:8:07-2- *Background of the project*

This section should provide a narrative description of the background to the project. Areas to be covered in the background are, inter alias:

- What is known about the problem to be dealt with?
- Why is the project necessary and why now?
- What experience has been gained previously within the project area?
- How are policy dialogue conducted with other parties i.e. the Government and other partners in the areas to be covered by the project?
- How is the project related to other actions in the civil society, UN family and the Government?
- What are the challenges facing achievement of results in the area to be addressed by the project?

8:8:07-3- Participants (Target group/s) of the project

This section of the PROPOSAL should introduce the groups and communities that the project will be approaching. Areas to be covered in the PROPOSAL include, inter alias:

- Which particular groups will the project approach?
- How are these groups selected?
- What is the geographic coverage of the project?
- In what way has the target group participated in the analysis of problems and goals?
- What are the expected gains for children in the short and long term?

8:8:07-4- Strategic approach

Briefly describe the strategic approach taken by the partner
Mention the principle government counterpart ministries and the level of
relationship (national, provincial, district)

8:8:07-5- Partnerships

Please list all partners with whom the organization will be collaborating to
achieve the goals of this proposal (i.e., local organizations being supported,
counterpart organizations, and donor partnerships)

8:8:07-6- Program Goals

> Describe the Goal

8:8:08- Program Objectives

> 8:8:08-1: Describe the Objective

> 8:8:08-2: Describe the Objective
> 8:8:08-3: Describe the Objective

8:8:09- Program activities

A brief overview of no more than 3 paragraphs summarizing the activities
that makes up the proposal

8:8:09- Activity Description

Restate each Objective with a description of each activity relating to the
Objective

Activities to Achieve Objective 1
Activity 1
Activity 2
Activity 3

Activities to Achieve Objective 2
Activity 1
Activity 2
Activity 3

Activities to Achieve Objective 3
Activity 1
Activity 2
Activity 3

8:8:10. **Management arrangements and reporting**

This section should outline the management and administrative arrangements for the project, including financial management and reporting.

8:8:11. Sustainability and Disengagement

This involves a description of mechanisms to ensure sustainability, other funding opportunities, hand over, involvement of government etc.

This section should describe the exit strategy or continuity/sustainability strategy of the project. It should provide a response to the following points, inter alias:

- What will happen after the sponsor support to this project has been phased out?
- Is the organization willing to take over the responsibility/ownership of the project in the long run? How?
- Will the organization have resources in the long run to carry out the project without the financial support of the sponsor?

8:8:12- PROJECT IMPLEMENTATION AND MANAGEMENT PLAN

8:8:12-1- Expected project results

the section should describe the overall results that the project is expected to. The discussion should also discuss whether there may be unintended effects of the project, and how these possibilities will be addressed.

The discussion should indicate in quantitative terms, to the extent possible, what the project will produce through its planned activities and budget.

8:8:12-1- Project activities and work plan

The section should describe how each immediate project objective will be carried out in terms of planned activities, their timing and duration, and who will be responsible for each activity. This can be summarized in a simple table.

8:8:12-3- Project Beneficiaries

this section describes who and how many people are expected to benefit from the project, both directly and indirectly. It should also discuss how intended beneficiaries have been involved in project design, and their expected role in project implementation and evaluation.

8:8:12-4- Implementing agent management of project

this section should describe:

- who will be responsible for planning and management of project operations as well as the roles of other bodies and organizations associated with the project
- What arrangements will be established to ensure that there will be effective coordination with other relevant programmers and activities?

The section should also discuss whether project operations are expected to continue, or expand to other areas or sectors, once the current phase of assistance is completed. This could include plans for introducing self-financing provisions to ensure continued viability of operations on project completion.

8:8:13- PROJECT MONITORING AND EVALUATION

This section should discuss proposed mechanisms and procedures for monitoring of project operations to ensure that activities occur as planned, that they remain directed towards stated objectives, and that appropriate corrective action is taken if required.

Specifically the discussion should indicate who will be responsible for preparing periodic project progress and final technical reports and for the accounting of expenditures made from the Voluntary Fund. All projects need to be evaluated on completion. This section should also identify the party who will responsible for this task as well as how intended beneficiaries will be involved.

8:8:14- BUDGET

An additional budget should be prepared to describe the budget components to be financed by Government, Project Implementing Agent and other parties participating in the project. This additional budget can be in local currency, but the equivalent in U.S. dollars should be indicated.

A description of the budget template line items and a budget template follow:

8:8:14-1- Project Personnel:

The resources of the Voluntary Fund can finance project personnel specialized needed to plan and carry out the project or specialized consultant services required to accomplish a specific project objective. Salaries and consultancy feeds should be reflective of local prevailing conditions. The Voluntary Fund does not prioritize projects with high personnel costs.

8:8:14-2- International Experts: for international personnel working for more than six months on the project. Job description/Terms of reference should be included in project document.

8:8l14-3- Consultants: for personnel working for less than six months on the project. Job description/Terms of reference should be included in project document.

8:8:14-4- Administrative Support: for clerical and related support tasks. Please note that financing of project support personnel is not a priority for the Voluntary Fund.

8:8:14-5- Official Travel of Project Personnel

8:8:14-6- National Professional Project Personnel. Job description/ Terms of reference should be included in project document.

8:8:15- Subcontracts:
This component pertains to specialized services provided the project by an outside contractor. Each subcontract will require a separate budget line; subcontractor terms of reference should be attached as an annex to the project document.

8:8:16- Training:

8:8:16-1- Group training and study tours: organized training programmers and study tours conducted outside the country of the project; group training normally does not exceed two months and study tours normally are one month or less

8:8:16-2- In service training: cost of individual and group training organized and conducted in the country of the project.

8:8:17- Equipment:

8:8:17-1- Expendable equipment: items of equipment, supplies or training materials

8:8:17-2- Non expendable equipment: items of equipment valued which have a serviceable life of five years or more.

8:8:17-3- Premises: The Voluntary Fund will not fund costs for premises (construction, rent, utilities). This line item should only be used to indicate any contributions from other donors, the government, or the implementing agent.

8:8:18- Miscellaneous:

8:8:18-1- Operation, Maintenance and Repair of Equipment: operation and maintenance of project equipment that cannot be covered by the host government or the project implementing agent

8:8:18-2- Publications and Report Costs: report costs, which may include the reproduction of a reasonable number of copies of project technical and final reports.

8:8:18-3- Sundry and Communications: official postage, communications and incidental supplies

CONCLUSION

The conceptualization and design of well-defined projects with excellent feasibility studies, appraisal, analysis and evaluation is of paramount importance for its effective and efficient implementation. But one crucial component is the sustainability of the project in this very competitive and challenging marketplace. But of more importance is the management of the various elements of sustainability put in place for the entire process.

The present society holds very high standards on any project having an impact on the standards of living of the citizens as well as other societal institutions and structures. The expectation is that projects should be defect-free, and they should be able to sustain itself for posterity, and that that project officials should be infallible and should be held accountable for any failed projects.

The recruitment of top-notch project professional with great potentials for high productivity has become the norm because of the great desire for sustainability. Standards for recruitment such as education, skills, knowledge, and work experience help to determine project sustainability. Also, training, encouragement of workplace diversity, career development, promotion and benefits are great motivational factors for project continuity. Employee assistance programs such as such as counseling, family assistance, therapy help to maintain a stable workforce.

The sustainability of projects should remain an integrated approach involving the social, economic, educational, legal, cultural and political components of the project. And this is the foundation of the Total Quality Management (TQM) and Project Sustainability Management (PSM) concepts.

APPENDIX:

GLOSSARY

A

Accountability- being answerable to one's superior in an organization for the exercise of one's authority and the performance of one's duties, being answerable for one's results.

Action Plan- A plans that describes what needs to be done and when it needs to be completed. It also a description of what needs to be done by who, when and how.

Administration- The aspect of the organization responsible for directing and managing the activities of the organization, program, project or major work packages

Administrative Management- Management that operates in the public trust, such as national, regional or local government administrations. It is often designed to survive indefinitely and the intended goal is to provide an environment acceptable to its constituents for their survival, prosperity and comfort.

Analysis- The study and examination of something complex and separation into more simple components- causes. variances, effects and impact and corrective action

Audit- A systematic examination of records and documents to determine adequacy and effectiveness in budgeting, accounting, financial and related policies and procedures

Authority- The legitimate power given to a person in an organization to utilize the resources to reach an objective and to exercise discipline.

B

Baseline- a planning and control instrument in the form of a summary attributes such as quantity, quality, timing, costs, etc that establishes a formal reference for comparison and verification of subsequent efforts, progress, analysis and control.

Break-Even Point- the productivity point at which value earned equals total cost.

Bureaucracy- A centralized system of administration for the conduct of business in a given field, usually highly structured and constrained by regulations, protocol, policies and procedures, and consequently is slow to react to change.

Business Engineering- A set of techniques that a company uses to design its business according to specific goals.

Business Reengineering- to perform business engineering where a comprehensive review of all business processes is undertaken in order to find completely new ways of restructuring them in order to achieve radical improvements.

C

Communication- The transmission and validated receipt of information so that the recipient understands what the senders intends, and the sender assures that the intent is understood.

Concept Study- Consideration of an idea that includes a review of its practicality, suitability, cost-effectiveness, etc. usually followed by a recommendation whether or not to proceed with the project.

Configuration- The technical description needed to build, test, accept, operate, install, maintain and support a system

Configuration Management- The process of designing, making and assembling the components of a project's deliverables in order to achieve the required functionality; the process of defining the configuration items in a system, controlling the release and change of those items throughout the project, recording and reporting the status of the configuration items and verifying their completeness. Its management process for establishing and maintaining consistency of a product or service performance, functional and physical attributes with its requirements, design and operational information throughout the process.

Contingency Planning- The development of managerial plans to be invoked in the event of specific risk events or that use alternative strategies to ensure project success if specific risk events occur

Continuous Quality Improvement- This is doing the right thing, doing it the right way, doing it right the first time and doing it on time.

Contract- A mutually binding agreement in which the contractor is obligated to provide services or products and the buyer is obligated to provide payment for them. Contracts fall into three categories: fixed price, cost reimbursable to unit price.

Culture- a pattern of artifacts, behaviors, values, beliefs, and assumptions that a group develops as it learns to cope with internal and external problems of survival and prosperity.

D

Development- The systematic use of scientific and technical knowledge in the design, development, test, and evaluation of a potential new product or service for the purpose of meeting specific performance requirements or objectives

Design- The process of developing and documenting a solution to a problem using technology experts and tools.

E

Effectiveness- A measure of the quality of attainment in meeting the objectives, the extent to which the goals of a project are attained, or the degree to which a system can be expected to achieve a set of specific requirements

Efficiency- A measures, (expressed as a percentage) of how well a process functions Efficiency is calculated by dividing the total time taken to complete a task by the product of the longest cycle time of the entire process and the number of workstation.

Empowerment- the enabling of project team members to achieve self-control to do their jobs with minimum supervision and with individual capabilities

Entrepreneur- A person who has the ability to see an opportunity, to obtain necessary capital, labor, and other inputs, and to know how to together an operation successfully, who has the willingness to take personal risks of success or failure.

F

Feasibility- The assessment of capability of being completed: the possibility, probability and suitability of accomplishment.

Feasibility Study- the methods and techniques used to examine technical and cost data to determine the economic potential and the practicality of project applications. This involves the analysis of variables such as interest rates, present worth factors, capitalization costs, operating costs, depreciation etc.

Flow Chart- A graphic means of depicting the steps or activities that constitute a process, often constructed from standard symbols representing a process or activity, decision, terminal, document flow lines, connector and terminal.

Functional Organization- An organizational structure in which staffs are grouped hierarchically by specialty e.g., production, marketing, engineering, accounting etc

G

General Manager- An executive level position responsible for integrating all project activities with the corporate strategic plan.

Goal- a statement of the strategic direction pursued by managers

H

Health System- An organization by which an individual or group's health is being managed for an effective and efficient service delivery

Health Insurance- The method of payment of a person's health benefits

Human Resources Management- The function of directing and coordinating human resources throughout the life of a project by applying the art and science of behavioral and administrative knowledge to achieve predetermined project objectives of scope, cost, time, quality and participant satisfaction.

Hypothesis- A supposition that is fully understood, that is not proven but assumed for purposes of argument

I

Implementation- The part of the project life cycle during which working drawings, specifications, and contract documents are prepared and contracts are tendered and awarded and the actual work undertaken

Implementation Planning- the process of converting all requirements into a logically sequenced set of project works authorizing agreements and subcontracts that define and authorize all work to be performed for the project.

Indicator- Information in a consistent format that points to a current status, trend or need for action.

Industrial Relations- An organizational function that deals with the relationships that exist between management personnel and the unions with organization

Information Management- The management of the systems, activities, and data that allows information in a project to be effectively acquired, stored, processed, accessed, communicated and archived.

Information System- A combination of personnel, efforts, forms, instructions, procedures, data, communication facilities and equipment that provide and organized and interconnected means for displaying information in support of specific functions.

Information Systems- A structured, interacting, complex of persons, machines and procedures designed to produce information which is collected from both internal and external sources for use as a basis for decision-making in specific contract/procurement activities.

Information Technology- Interconnected systems and equipment used in automated acquisition, storage, manipulation, management, movement, control, display, switching, interchange, transmission, or reception of data or information.

ISO 900 series standards- A set of related international standards on quality management and quality assurance developed to help companies effectively document the quality system element to be implemented to maintain an efficient quality system in a project or operation. These standards, initially developed in 1987 are not specific to any particular industry, product or service. The International Organization developed the standards for Standardization (ISO), a specialized agency for standardization composed of national standards boards of over 91 countries.

J

Job Description- Written outline of skills, responsibilities, knowledge, authority, environment and interrelationships involved in an individual's job.

K

Key Performance Indicators- Project management factors that are determined at the beginning of the project, reflect on the key objectives of the project provide the basis for project management trade-off decisions, measurable to reflect the critical success factors of the project.

L

Law- A binding custom or practice of a community enforced by the judiciary, a rule of conduct or action prescribed or formally recognized as binding or enforced by a controlling authority.

Leadership- The ability to set goals and objectives and generating enthusiasm and motivation amongst project team members and stakeholders to work towards these objectives

Logistics- The business of planning and carrying out the movement and maintenance of resources to accomplish a particular task.

M

Management- The process of planning, organizing, executing, coordinating, monitoring, forecasting and exercising control to make sure that results are obtained according to established performance standards for scope, quality, time and cost

Management Information System- a system dedicated to increasing the effectiveness of the organization by implementing computer-based data retrieval, presentation systems and productivity tools.

Mission- The fundamental purpose of an organization in terms of customer need, core product or service, target markets, and technology used to satisfy the need stated in a way that sets the organization apart from others of its type.

Monitoring- The act of overseeing the progress of a project or activity, and of ensuring that it is conducted, recorded and reported in conformity with the quality standards and protocol set.

N

Networking- The exchange of information or services among individuals, groups or organizations

O

Objective- A quantified business or corporate level performance target to be reached in a specified time frame.

Operation- Work performed by people and machines on materials or information; it transforms input into output; includes operational tasks for doing the work and operational methods guiding the work.

Organization- A company, corporation, firm or enterprise whether incorporated or not, public or private

Organizational Structure- A structure that defines the reporting relationships, processes, systems and procedures of a project

P

Paradigm- The organizational realities such as values, beliefs, traditional practices, methods, tools, that make members of the social group construct to integrate the thoughts and actions of its members. It provides rules and standards of management practice, laws, theories, applications, and instrumentation.

Paradigm Shift- when many beliefs and actions change in concert within an organization.

Performance- A quantitative and qualitative measure characterizing a physical or functional attribute relating to the execution of an operation or function Performance attributes include (how many or how much) quality, (how well) coverage (how much area, how far), timelines (how responsive, how frequent), and readiness (availability, mission/operational readiness). Performance is an attribute for all systems, people, products, services and processes including those for development, production, verification, deployment, operation, support, training and disposal. Thus supportability parameters, manufacturing process variability, reliability etc are all performance measures.

Policies- General statements or principles intended to guide individual thinking, decision-making and action.

Process- The flow of products, material, or information from one worker or operation to another to transport input into output for consumers: composed of four phenomena: - processing, inspection, transport and delay.

Problem Solving- Finding the cause of a problem and addressing the cause so that the problem does not return.

Project Sustainability Management (PSM) - A process designed to customize sustainable development project goals and indicators to suit local conditions and priorities. It is also a framework designed to ensure that a project's sustainability goals are aligned and traceable to recognized and accepted whole society goals, objectives and priorities.

Protocol- *A document that describes the objectives, design, methodology, statistical considerations and organization of a project*

Q

Quality- a principle that encourages excellence in everything: - products, strategies, systems, processes and people. It advocates for accuracy, efficiency and effectiveness, appropriateness and patient satisfaction.

Quality Control- Activities directed towards monitoring instruments and test procedures, testing systems monitored so that the test results are valid and making sure that accurate statistics are used to validate results: the process of monitoring specific project results to determine if they comply with relevant standards and identifying ways to eliminate causes of unsatisfactory performance.

Quality Assurance- a program in which overall activities conducted are directed towards assuring quality of products and services provided: the development of a comprehensive program which includes the processes of identifying objectives and strategy, of client interaction and of organizing and coordinating planned and systematic controls for maintaining established standards.

Quality Audit- A systematic, independent examination and review to determine whether quality activities and related results comply with planned arrangements and whether these arrangements are implemented effectively and are suitable to achieve the objectives.

R

Research- Studious inquiry or examination, investigation or experimentation aimed at the discovery and interpretation of facts, or the revision of accepted theories or laws in the light of a fact.

Resource- any variable capable of definition that is required for the completion of an activity and may constrain the project Resources can be people, equipment, facilities, funding or anything needed to perform work in a project.

S

Sustainability- A systematic concept relating to the continuity of economic, social, institutional and environmental aspects of human society as well as the non-human environment.

System- this consists of an integrated collection of personnel, knowledge, abilities, motivation, equipment, machinery, methods, measures, processes, and task activities designed to achieve repetitive or reproducible results.

Strategy- The pattern of organizational moves and managerial approaches used to achieve organizational objectives and pursue the organizational mission.

Strategic Management- the process managers use to formulate and implement strategies for providing best customer value that will the objectives of the organization.

Syndrome- A group of related or coincident events, actions, or situations: a pattern of circumstances, signs, or indications, which characterize a particular social, economic or political condition.

T

Technology- The element of applied science needed to provide value in the goods and services produced: a manner of completing a task using technical processes, methods or knowledge

Total Quality Management (TQM) - It is a people-focused management system that aims at continual increase in customer satisfaction at continually lowers real cost: a system for identifying what clients want, defining the organization's mission, measuring throughout the whole process how well performance meets the required standards and involving the total organization in the implementation of a deliberate policy of continuous improvement.

U

Unemployment Rate- The proportion of the workforce, which has either lost employment in the past month, or has active sought jobs unsuccessfully during that time

Utility- The ability of a product to satisfy a consumer's needs.

V

Value Management- a structured means of improving effectiveness in line with the organization's goals .It refers to the overall process of identifying key issues and setting targets, identifying the teams and processes necessary to achieve these and implementing them to obtain positive results

Value Management Study- a function-oriented appraisal of all elements of an item, system or process to achieve essential characteristics at minimum overall cost. This procedure involves information gathering, function analysis, creative solution generation, judgmental solution evaluation, and development of alternatives, presentation of recommendations and approval, implementation of changes and follow-up reporting of results.

W

Work- The expenditure of effort, physical or mechanical in the cause of an activity or task: the performance of any service for which payment is to be made.

X

Y

Z

STRATEGIC IMPLEMENTATION TRAINING FORMS

1) DAILY ORGANIZER

DATE: / /

TIME	ACTIVITY	OUTCOME
6:00		
:30		
7:00		
:30		
8:00		
:30		
9:00		
:30		
10:00		
:30		
11:00		
:30		
12:00		
:30		

2) WEEKLY ORGANIZER

WEEK ENDING:

DATE:

TIME	MON	TUES	WEDS	THURS	FRI	SAT	SUN
6:00							
:30							
7:00							
:30							
8:00							
:30							
9:00							
:30							
10:00							
:30							
11:00							
:30							
12:00							
:30							

3) MONTHLY ORGANIZER

MONTH OF

DAY	MORNING	AFTERNOON	EVENING
1			
2			
3			
4			
5			
6			
7			
8			
9			
10			
11			
12			
13			
14			

COMMENTS:

4) CUSTOMER CONTACT SHEET

#	NAME	ADDRESS	PHONE	FAX	EMAIL	WEBSITE
1						
2						
3						
4						
5						
6						
7						
8						
9						
10						
11						
12						
13						
14						

COMMENTS:

5) GOALS/OBJECTIVES SHEET

#	GOAL/ OBJECTIVE	TIMEFRAME	ASSESSMENT	OUTCOME	NEXT PLAN
1					
2					
3					
4					
5					
6					
7					
8					
9					
10					
11					
12					
13					
14					

COMMENTS:

6) QUALITY IMPROVEMENT STRUCTURE:

<u>Organizational Leadership</u>

Executive

Quality Council

Quality Boards

<u>Process Leadership</u>

Improvement Teams

(Cross Functional)

(Departmental)

(Self-Directed)

<u>Project Leadership</u>

Work Groups

<u>Empowered Individuals</u>

Self-managed People

7) PROCESS IMPROVEMENT TEAMS:

CRITERIA	CROSS FUINCTIONAL	DEPARTMENTAL
Purpose	Improve processes spanning two or more departments	Improve operations within department
Size	5 - 8 members	7 – 10 members
Composition	Organization-wide representation	Department employees
Selection	Quality Council Priority first	Department Manager Team Managers
Accountable To	Quality Council	Department Manager
Average Life Cycle	12 – 24 meetings	Indefinite
Meeting Duration	1 - 2 hours	1 – 2 hours
Data Collection and Summarization	Team assignment Staff support	Team assignment Staff support
Implementation	Quality Council Department Managers	Department Managers Team Managers

8) ROLES AND RESPONSIBILITIES:

The neutral servants of the team are the Facilitator and Recorder. Both practice techniques to get the Team's picture, while staying out of the picture.

CRITERIA	FACILITATOR	RECORDER
Purpose	To promote effective group dynamics	Capture group memory
Major concern	How decisions are made	How decisions are made
Principle responsibilities	Ensure equal participation by team members Mediate and resolve conflicts Provide feedback and support team leaders Suggest problem-solving techniques and tools Provide quality training No ownership in outcome	Record long-term and short-term group memory Instant record, easy reference Content, process recorded What, when, who captured Support facilitator No ownership in outcome
Position type	Organization-wide (Neutral)	Organization-wide (Neutral)
Selection	Personal characteristics	Technical capabilities

9) DEVELOPING MEETING GROUND RULES:

ATTENDANCE

Who will schedule meeting, arrange for room, and notify members?

How will absences be handled?

Can team members be replaced for absenteeism?

TIME MANAGEMENT

How does the team define "on time"? Are starting and ending times enforced?

How will time allotted to agenda items be monitored?

What is the role of the timekeeper? Who will serve as timekeeper?

PARTICIPATION

What advance preparation is expected?

How will participation be monitored to ensure equal contributions?

How will activities be monitored to ensure productive meetings?

How are assignments made? What are the expectations for their completion?

COMMUNICATION

How did candid can members be? Is information confidential to team?

How will discussions be started? What if discussions get off track?

How will interruptions or side conversations be handled?

What listening skills are expected?

What forms of criticism are acceptable?

How will creativity be encouraged and negative thinking discouraged?

DECISION MAKING

How will differences of opinion be expressed and resolved?

How will conflicts among members be handled?

What process will be used to reach consensus? To guard against "group think"?

How will decisions be made?

DOCUMENTATION

What process will be used to set meeting agendas and allocate time?

How will agendas and minutes be distributed?

Who will serve as recorder of minutes?

Where will documentation be kept?

OTHER

What meeting interruptions are acceptable and non-acceptable?

How will breaks be handled?

10) MEETING GROUND RULES:

Team Name _____ Date _____

ATTENDANCE _____
_____
_____

TIME MANAGEMENT: _____
_____
_____

COMMUNICATION: _____
_____
_____

DECISION MAKING: _____
_____
_____

DOCUMENTATION: _____
_____
_____

OTHER: _____
_____
_____

11) DRAFTING A TEAM CHARTER

TEAM MISSION

What parts of the process or system should be studied?
What led to selection of this issue?
What data exists or is required to study the issue?

EXPECTED IMPROVEMENTS

What are the goals or expected outcomes of this study?
What magnitude of improvement is expected?
Who will approve and implement recommendations?

BOUNDARIES AND CONSTRAINTS

What parts of the process or system should not be studied?
What time or budgetary constraints are applicable?
What decision-making authority does the team have?

RESORUCES AVAILABLE

What internal or external experts should be consulted?
Who may be called upon to assist the team?
What support services are available such as computers, graphics, presentation materials, etc?
Who will cover for members during meetings?

TEAM REPRESENTATION

What functional areas will be represented?
What job titles members will represent?

12) TEAM CHARTER:

TEAM NAME: _____ DATE: _____

MISSION: _____

_____

_____

EXPECTED IMPROVEMENTS: _____

_____

_____

_____

BOUNDARIES AND CONSTRAINTS: _____

_____

_____

RESOURCES AVAILABALE; _____

_____

_____

TEAM REPRESENTATION: _____

_____

_____

_____

13) MEETING AGENDA:

_____ DATE: _____

STARTING TIME: ENDING TIME:

Agenda Item		Action Discussion Information	Person Responsible	Time Needed
1. Read Minutes from Previous Meeting.		I	Team	
2. Review Meeting Agenda		I, D	Team	
3.				
4				
5.				
6.				
7.				
8.				
9.				
10.				
11. Review Team processes				
Set agenda for next meeting		D	Team	

14) MINUTES RECORD

TEAM: _____ DATE: _____

STARTING TIME: _____ ENDING TIME; _____

Members Present
1.
2.
3.
4.
5.
6.
7.
8.

Key Discussion Points (attach documents as necessary)

Decisions and Action Items (attach documents as necessary)

Next steps

Next Meeting Date _____ Time _____ Place _____

Committed by _____ approved by _____

　　　　　　　Recorder　　　　　　　　　　　　Team Leader

15) ATTENDANCE LOG:

TEAM: DATE TEAM CHARTERED:

Meeting Date

Member name

COMMENTS:

NEXT MEETING DATE:

16) TEAM PROJECT RECORD

Project Name _____ Date: _____

_____

DESCRIPTION: _____

_____

REASON FOR SELECTION (CURRENT STATE): _____

_____

EXPECTED IMPROVEMENTS (FUTURE STATE): _____

_____

_____

PEOPLE/PROCESSES IMPACTED BY IMPLEMENTATION: ___

_____

_____

RESOURCES REQUIRED (PEOPLE, FINANCIAL, EQUIPMENT): _

_____

_____

_____

RESULTS: _____

_____

_____

TEAM REPRESENTATION: _____

_____

PROJECT BEGAN: PROJECT ENDED   REPORTED BY

19) EMPLOYEE SATISFACTION SURVEY

1- Expectation from the job
2- Freedom to do the job
3- Information about the organization
4- Role in the organization
5- Fairness to employees
6- Empowerment of Employees
7- Creation and encouragement of an atmosphere of trust
8- Credit and Praise
9- Fulfillment of Career goals
10- Job Security
11- Company Benefit Programs
12- Services to External Customers
13- Knowledge of the problems and potentials of the company
14- Accomplishment of the company
15- Cooperation between employees
16- Safety and health procedures
17- In-Service training
18- Available resources
19- Rules and Procedures- applicability
20- Employee satisfaction

20)-PROBLEM-SOLVING TECHNIQUES

Fundamental journalistic questions to identify, analyze and evaluate situations are:

Who? When? What? Where? And how?

Some Problem solving issues and questions are:-

#	ISSUE	QUESTIONS
1	Problem Identification	What is the main problem? What are the causes? How does it affect the organization? How can it be addressed or remedied?
2	Planning	What needs to be done first? How will it be done? What resources are needed to accomplish the task? Who will do what in the task? What are the alternative strategies for the problem?
3	Information Use	What information is needed for the problem? What do you know about it? What are other sources of information?
4	Total Picture	What led to the problem? How did it happen? What has been tried so far? What has been made of this so far? When does this usually happen
5	Description of Issue	What is the problem like? Tell me more about it. What actually happened?
6	Exploration of Problem	Why do you think things are done like this? How can this type of problem be handled? What choices exist for this problem?
7	Clarification of Problem	How does this make sense to you? What is confusing about this problem? What does it really mean to the organization?
8	Exploiting Alternatives	What possibilities exist for solutions? If any choices, what can be done?
9	Evaluation of Problem	How do you feel about the problem? What do you think is the best thing to do?

21) COMPONENTS OF STRUCTURE, PROCESS AND OUTPUT

STRUCTURE
1- Facilities
2- Equipment
3- Supplies
4- Human Resources
5- Financial Resources
6- Management Systems
    - Job Description
    - Appointment Control
    - Employee Policies
    - Client Policies

PROCESS
1- Assessment
2- Analysis/Diagnosis
3- Treatment Planning
4- Treatment
5- Implementation
6- Client Management
7- Informed Consent
8- Referrals
9- Progress/Status Report
10- Customer Input
11- Monitoring and Evaluation

OUTPUT
1- Management Status
2- Technical Quality
3- Treatment Completion
4- Functional Status
5- Customer Satisfaction
6- Maintenance
7- Cost Savings
8- Output Status

COMMON BUSINESS JARGONS

A

Ace- An expert; a person who is very good at something

B

Baby Boomers- People who were born between 1945 and 2964

Baby Bust Generation- The generation following baby boomers when the birth rate was low

Back in the saddle- In control again

Backfire- to produce results opposite of those expected

Backlash effect- A negative reaction by the individual or group subject to an action

Bailouts- Assistance, often financial

Bargain basement levels- lowest, inexpensive, cheap

Bankroll- Finance a business deal, the sum of money an individual possesses

Bargaining chip- A negotiation ploy, usually a demand which the negotiator plans to give up getting something more intensely desired

Beat around the bush- Avoid getting to the point

Behind the wheel- in control

Bells and whistles- features

The big picture- overall or larger view of things

Big Ticket items- items costing large sums of money

Big wheel- important person, manager

Black Market- illegal buying and selling of products

Blockbuster- a smashing success

Blow the whistle- stop some activity by reporting its occurrence

Blue chip- top of the line, highest, best form

Blue Collar worker- Non-professional employee, laborer, unskilled worker-often working in factories and not wearing suites or ties

Blue sky- Have little more than just hopes and dreams

Bombshell- big event, surprising event

Bottom line- An accounting of profit and loss, the money a company keeps after paying the bills, the main idea or point, purpose or essence

Brainpower- knowledge

Brainstorm- form of creative thinking, often done in groups, in wild ideas are sought without regard to their practicality-judgment of idea quality is withheld until after the creative part is completed

The brass- top management

Breakthrough- dramatically new product or idea

Buckle down- get down to work, stop fooling around

Button downs/pin-strips- corporate dress, suit and tie, also refer to people who wear such clothing

Burning the power trail- rapidly moving information flow

Buying power- ability to purchase

By the book/number- follow the rules

C

Calling all the shots- making important decisions

Catch 22- an irresolvable contradiction

CEO- Chief Executive Officer, head of the company, boss

Clone- duplicate, make copies of, imitate

Competitive edge- ability to compete quickly and efficiently, advantage

Cornerstone- foundation, indispensable part

Corporate elite- top executive

Corporate takeover- one company buying another

A coup in- major marketing idea

Cowboy economy- uses resources and then moves on

CYA- covers your assessment; protect yourself from repercussions or blame

D

Deep pockets- companies or investors with a lot of money to spend

Down the drain- something wasted, thrown out, wasted, gone, and lost

Down the wire- last minute, completed just before the deadline

Downside- negative

Downsize- cutting back on jobs and services to save money

Downtime- period of inactivity

Draw a picture- explain in detail

E

Early bird session- very early morning meeting
Easy as A, B, C- very simple
Economic giant- corporate or business leader
Eleventh hour- at the very last minute, no time left, just before a deadline
Endangered species- may be in jeopardy, may be eliminated
Entrepreneurial spirit- eagerness to take business risks
Executive suite- top management position

F

Fallout- by products of a decision
Fast-track- the way to rapid promotion or success
Feedback-response
Fiscal year- year for accounting purposes (does not necessarily begin in January)
Fishbowl- in the public eye
Flop- a failed product or marketing campaign
Follow through- finish, complete the task
From scratch- from the beginning
Fruits of your labor- money, land, property, things you worked to acquire

G

Game plan- a marketing strategy, plan for a product, campaign etc
Garbage in garbage out- output can be no better than input
Gimmick- a special feature or item in a marketing plan designed to increase the appeal of a product
Global arena- world marketplace
Gray market- legal but unauthorized distribution channel
Green light- signal to go ahead, proceed
Greenpeace- a group fighting for environmental issues

H

Hands-on management- management directly involved in employees activities

Heydays- in good times

Hidden cost- expense not easy to measure in financial terms

Hierarchical command- traditional, authoritative, top to bottom

High end- more expensive, highly priced

Honeymoon- good relations: enhanced state of cooperation usually found at the beginning of a business relationship

I

Infant industry- new manufacturing companies

In the black- operate profitably

In the red- operate at a loss

In the driver's seat- in charge

J

Jump on the bandwagon- join what is popular, be one of the "in crowds"

K

Know how- knowledge, smarts

L

Labor intensive- production requiring a lot of workers

Leaps and bounds- large jumps, amounts or quantities

Level playing field- to be treated the same as everyone

Liquid- convertible into cash quickly, having a lot of cash

Living on borrowed time- existing/operating in a very precarious situation

Loopholes- legal ways to get around the law

Lump-sum payments- pay all a t once

M

Melt down- product failure

Mission-oriented- dedicated to accomplishing the goal

N

Niche marketing- serving a unique market segment better the larger competitors

O

Off-the shelf/rack- made to standard specifications, readily available at the source of supply, not custom made
Offshore producers- foreign overseas companies
Overrun- production in excess of requirements, often must be sold at low prices

P

Pendulum swing- Play the float- write a check today, deposit money tomorrow
Pool of applicants- potential employees
Pros and cons- the benefits and disadvantages, the good and the bad
Publicity stunt- outrageous act to get public attention and media coverage

Q

Quality circles- groups that focus on quality improvement
Quick buck- money made fast

R

Rake in- bring in large amounts, usually money
Renegade- maverick, one who refuses to conform to norms
Rest on his laurels- sit back, relax based on previous successes
Root cause- primary reason
Rubber stamp- to O.K, without really studying the situation

S

Sailed through- successful completion with no obstacles
Satellite offices- branch offices
Scam- rip-off scheme, to cheat someone out of something
Shadow organization- second, behind the scene
Shop floor employees- lower level employees
Shotgun approach- without a specific target, haphazard

Siphoned off- remove or take, usually money
Skyrocketing- increasing dramatically
Star status- honor, celebrity
State-of-the art- modern, up-to date
Streamlining- cutting back
Strongholds- powerful areas
Survival of the fittest- those able to adjust to life will survive (Darwinism)
Sweatshops- unhealthy place to work, usually paying low wages and hiring illegal workers

T

To pull off- successfully accomplishing something
Top notch- the best, most important
Track record- past performance
Turning point- the beginning of a new time era

U

Unbridled optimism- uncontrolled enthusiasm, feeling good
Undercutting- pricing lower
Upscale- superior, better quality, often more expensive

V

Voting stock- right to vote on the company's business

W

Wage freeze- no raises on employee earnings
White collar- executives, managers, professional employees
White collar crimes- crimes committed by professional workers
White knight- good guy
Written off- given up on; in accounting, to remove assets from balance sheet because they no longer have value

X

Y

Yuppie- young professional person

Z

A zillion dollars- lots and lots of money

COMMON BUSINESS ACRONYMS

AAMOF- As a Matter of Fact
ADDIE- Analysis, Design, Development, Implementation, Evaluation
AFAIK- As Far As I Know
ASAP- As Soon As Possible
BEER- Behavior, Effect, Expectation, Results
BPR- Business Process Re-engineering
BTW- By the Way
CIPP- Context, Input, Process, Product
CP- Change Proposal
CPI- Continuous Process Improvement
CPM- Critical Path Method
DMP- Data Management Plan
DTP- Detailed Test Plan
EAC- Estimate at Completion
EOD- End of Discussion
ERIC- Educational Resource Information Center
FAS- Feasibility Analysis Study
FY- Fiscal Year
FYI- For Your Information
GIGO- Garbage in Garbage Out
HR- Human Resources
HRD- Human Resource Department
IAW- In Accordance With
IDT- Integrated Development Team
IMHO- In My Humble Opinion
INPO- In No Particular Order
I/O- Input/output
IOW- In Order Words
IQ- Intelligence Quotient
ISPI- International Society for Performance Improvement
ISO- International Standards Organization

JITT- Just In Time Training
KM- Knowledge Management
LO- Learning Objective
LRC- Learning Resource Center
OJT- On the Job Training
OSHA- Occupational Safety and Health Administration
OTOH- On the Other Hand
PA_ Performance Assessment
PE- Practical Exercise
PERT- Program Evaluation and Review Technique
PMP- Program Management Plan
PPP- Personal Performance Profile
QA- Quality Assurance
QC- Quality Council
QI- Quality Improvement
QM- Quality Management
R&D- Research and Development
RESA- Research, Evaluation and System Analysis
RFI- Request for Information
SA- Situational Analysis
SMART- Specific, Measurable, Achievable, Relevant and Time based
SME- Subject Matter Expert
SOO- Statement of Objectives
SOS- Save Our Ship
SWOT- Strengths, Weaknesses, Opportunities, Threats
SPEC- Specification
STD- Standard
STM- Short Term Memory
TADS- Training Analysis Data Sheet
TBA- To Be Announced
TBD- To Be Determined
TEE- Training Effectiveness Evaluation
TEMP- Test and Evaluation Master Plan
TINSTAAFL- There Is No Such Thing as a Free Lunch

TQM- Total Quality Management
TR- Training Requirement
WBS- Work Breakdown Structure
WIIFM- What Is In For Me
WYSIWYG- What You See IS What You Get
YOYO- You're On Your Own
YTD- Year to Date
ZD- Zero Defects

BIBLIOGRAPHY

Argenti, Paul A. *The Portable MBA Desk Reference: An Essential Business companion.* John Wiley & Sons Inc. 1994.

Bounds, Greg. *Beyond Total Quality Management: toward the Emerging Paradigm.* McGraw-Hill Inc., New York, 1994.

Kushel, Gerald. *Reaching the Peak Performance Zone.* American Management Association, New York, 1994.

Waitley, Denis. *Empires of the Mind: Lessons to Lead and succeed in a Knowledge-based World.* William Morron and Company Inc. New York, 1995.

Bechtel, Michele L. *The Management Compass.* American Management Association, New York, NY, USA, 1995.

Marshall, Edward M.D. *Transforming the Way We Work: The Power of the Collaborative Work Place.* American Management Association, New York, 1995.

MacDonald, John. *Calling a Halt to Mindless Change: A Plea for Common Sense Management.* American Management Association International. New York, 1997.

Drucker, Peter F. *Managing in Turbulent Times.* Harper & Row, Publishers, New York, 1980.

Meredith, Jack R. *Project Management. A Management Approach.* Second Edition. John Wiley & Sons, Inc., 1985.

TQM: Total Quality Management Diagnostics. http://www.skyenet. net/~leg/tqm.htm

Sarabok, Karen. *Project Management 1: Planning and Scheduling.* Project Excel Corporation, Hummelstown, Pennsylvania, 1980

Sarabok, Karen. *Project Management 11: Cost, Evaluation and_Control*. Project Excel Corporation, Hummelstown, Pennsylvania, 1988

Wideman, R. Max. Wideman's Comparative Glossary of project Management Terms, v2.1, May 2001.www.pmforum.org/library/glossary/PMG_A00.htm.

Overview of the ISO System. www.iso.org/iso/en/aboutiso/introduction/index.html

Hansen, Dexter, A., Total Quality Management (TQM) Tutorial/Help Page (Overview). March 2005. www.home.att.net/~iso9k1/tqm.html

Integrated Quality Diagnostics, Inc. TQM: The 9 TQM tools, The 9 TQM SPC Tools. www.iqd.com/pfttools.htm

Human Resource Management.www.managementhelp.org/hr_mgmnt/hr_mgnt.htm

Research and Practice in Human Resource Management. www.rphrm.curtin.edu.au/1994/issue/tqm.html

Project Management Principles.www.hyperthot.com/pm_princ.htm

SWOT Analysis. www.businessballs.com/swotanalysisfreetemplate.htm

SWOT Analysis. www.en.wikipedia.org/wiki/SWOT_analysis

SWOT Analysis. www.marketingteacher.com/Lessons/lesson_swot.htm

Leadership. www.en.wikipedia.org/wiki/Leadership

Wikipedia: http://en.wkipedia.org/wiki/Wikipedia

Capacity Building- www.en.wikipedia.org/wiki/Capacity_building

Knowledge Management. www.en.wikipedia.org/wiki/Knowledge_management

Knowledge Management. www.systems-thinking.org/kmgmt/kmgmt.htm

Knowledge Praxis. www.media-access.com/whatis.htm

Carnegie Mellon Software Engineering Institute, Six Sigma. www.sei.cmu.edu/str/descriptions/sigma6_body.html

Six Sigma. www.en.wikipedia.org/wiki/Six_Sigma

Business Process Management-Sustainable Business Rules: An Introduction, www.bpminstitute.org/articles/article/article/sustainable-business-rules

University of Colorado. www.colorado.edu/AMStudies/lewis/ecology/making.htm

Msnbc Broadcasting Company: www.Msnbc.com/id/22340448/

Morfaw, John. Total Quality Management: A Model for the Sustainability of Projects and Programs in Africa, University Press of America, 2009, (Chapters. 2, 3, 4, 5, 11, 12)

Six Sigma- Wikipedia, the free encyclopedia, www.en.wikipedia.org/wiki/Six_Sigma

ICT Regulation, www.ictregulationtoolkit.org/en/Section.3306.html

MandE NEWS, Planning for Monitoring and Project Sustainability: A Guideline on concepts, issues and tools: www.mande.co.uk/docs//khan.htm

The Finance Project, 1401 New York Ave, NW, Suite 800, Washington DC, 20005;

Sustainability Planning: Key to Success: www.financeproject.org

Project Management-Wikipedia, the free encyclopedia: www.wikipedia.org/wiki/Project_management

Sustainability-Wikipedia, the free encyclopedia: www.wikipedia.org/wiki/sustainability

Project Failure Statistics: www.it-cortex.com/Stat_Failure_Cause.htm

Thomsett International: Project Pathology; www.thomsettinternational.com/main/articles/path/patholo

Sustainable Development Triangle: www.eoearth.org/article/Sustainable_development_triangle

International Institute for Sustainable Development. Business Strategy for Sustainable Development: Leadership and Accountability for the 1990s, 1992

Wallace, A William. Project Sustainability Management: A Roadmap for Sustainable Development

Taylor, Tom. A Sustainability Checklist for Managers of Projects; PM World Today- January 2008 (Vol. X, issue 1)

Boswell, Peter. Project Sustainability Management: A Systems Approach, FIDIC, Geneva, PGB, July, 2005

American Evaluation Association-Wikipedia, the free encyclopedia www.wikipedia.org/wiki/America_Evaluation_Association

Monitoring and Evaluation for Grant Schemes, Local Partnership for Employment, Croatia, an EU funded project CARDS 2002.

Janet Shapiro, Monitoring and Evaluation, CIVICUS, Southdale, 2135, South Africa
www.civicus.org
United Nations Population Fund, Program Manager's Planning Monitoring and Evaluation Toolkit, 10017

Project Management Institute (PMI), Project Management Journal, Volume 42, Number 1, February 2011, (pp.15-16)
Sustainable Society Foundation (SSF), Wassenaarseweg 16, 2596 CH, The Hague, The Netherlands, www.sssfindex.com/framework
McLeish, Kenneth, Ed., Bloomsbury Guide to Human Thought: Ideas that Shaped the World, Bloomsbury Publishing Limited, 2 Soho Square, London, W1V, 5DE, 1993, (p p. 724),
Project Management Institute. *Guide to the Project management Body of Knowledge* (PMBOK Guide) - Fourth Edition, Project Management Institute Inc., Newtown Square, Pennsylvania, 2008
Bill Wallace. *FIDIC Project Sustainability Management* II, Version # 1, July 7th, 2005
Capek, Barbara. *Sustainable Development Projects: Development of a Categorization*, PM World Today, August 2010, Vol. x11, issue V111

INDEX

A

Accountability, 139
Acronyms, 177–179
Action Plan, 139
Administration, 139
Administrative Management, 139
Affinity diagrams, 34
American Evaluation Association (AEA), 107
Analysis, 139
Anthony, William P., 76
Audit, 139
   pre-assessment, 65–66
Authority, 140
Awareness program, 61

B

Bar charts, 39
Baseline, 140
Bechtell, Michele L., 76–77
"Bill of Rights for the Planet," xviii, 4–5
Break, 140
Bridges, William, 77
Brundtland, Gro Harlem, xvii
Brundtland Commission, 3
Brundtland Report, xvii
Budget, 134
   development, 61
Bureaucracy, 140
Business acronyms, 177–179
Business Engineering, 140

Business jargon, 170–176
Business Plan, 123–124
   business competition, 124
   business location, 124
   business personnel, 124
   description of the business, 123
   financial information, 124–125
   managing the business, 124
   market description, 124
   purpose of the business, 123
Business Reengineering, 140

C

Capacity Building, xix, 99–100
   agents, 100
   examples, 99
Cause and effect charts, 37
Change Management Process, 121–122
Charts
   bar, 39
   cause and effect, 37
   control, 41
   Gantt, 36
   Pareto, 38
   pie, 40
   process decision, 36
   process flow, 31–32
   run, 39
Communication, 140
   channels, 28
   management, 15

Concept Study, 140
Configuration, 140
Configuration Management, xix,
96–97, 140–141
Contingency Planning, 141
Continuous Quality Improvement
(CQI), xix, 26, 66–68, 73, 141
Contract, 141
Control charts, 41
Cost-benefit analysis, 109
Cost-effectiveness analysis, 109
Cost management, 14
Crosby, Philip B., 83
Culture, 141
changes, 80
of total quality management, 85–87
Customer contact sheet, 153

D
Daily organizer, 150
Data sheets, 38
Deming, Dr. W. Edwards, 71, 81–82
Design, 141
Development, 141
Diagrams
affinity, 34
matrix, 35
relationship, 36
scatter, 41
tree, 35
Drucker, Peter F., 78

E
Economic development indicators,
110
Effectiveness, 141–142
Efficiency, 142
Employees
empowerment, 1–2
satisfaction survey, 167
Empowerment, 1–2, 142

Entrepreneur, 142
Evaluation, 106–113, 134
characteristics, 108
designing the process, 113
difference between monitoring
and, 112
indicators, 110–112
objectives, 107–108
types, 109

F
Facilitators, 46
training, 62
Feasibility, 142
Feasibility Study, 142
background, 119
business options, 120
business requirements, 120
current business problems, 120
current business review, 119
Executive Summary, 119
process, 119–120
Flow Chart, 142
Formative evaluation, 109
Functional Organization, 142

G
Gantt charts, 36
General Manager, 142
Goal, 142
Goals/objectives sheet, 154

H
"Hannover Principles," xviii
Health Insurance, 143
Health System, 143
Histograms, 40
Human Resources Management, 15,
143
components, 97–98

Humphrey, Albert S., 103
Hypothesis, 143

I

Implementation, 143
Implementation Planning, 143
Indicator, 143
Industrial Relations, 143
Information, Communication and
    Technology (ICT), 2
Information Management, 143
Information System, 143
Information Systems, 144
Information Technology, 144
International Organization for
    Standardization (ISO), total
    quality control and, 94–96
Ishikawa, Kaoru, 84
ISO 900 series standards, 144

J

Jargon, 170–176
Job Description, 144
Juran, Joseph M., 82–83

K

Key Performance Indicators, 144
Knowledge Management, xix, 100–
    102
disciplines and technologies, 102
processes, 101
programs, 101

L

Law, 144
Leadership, 145
    commitment, 80
    quality, 89–90
Logistics, 145

M

MacDonald, John, 77
Management, 145
    differences between traditional
        and total quality
        management, 50
    individual skills, 68
    review, 65
    traditional compared with
        integrated, 47–48
Management Information System,
    145
Marketing Plan, 125
Marshall, Edward E., 78
Matrix diagrams, 35
Meetings
    agenda form, 163
    attendance log form, 165
    developing ground rules, 158–160
    minutes record form, 164
Mission, 145
Models
    for International Organization for
        Standardization (ISO),
        95–96
    strategic planning, 56
Monitoring, 106–113, 134, 145
    characteristics, 108
    designing the process, 113
    difference between evaluation and,
        112
    indicators, 110–112
Monthly organizer, 152

N

National Society for Professional
    Engineers (NSPE), 73
Neblock, Paul, 77
Networking, 145

O

Objective, 145
Operation, 145
Organization, 146
Organizational Structure, 42–50, 146
  cross-functional teams, 44–45
  departmental teams, 45
  development, 59–60
  example, 42
  Executive Council, 43
  integrated, 49–50
  Quality Council, 43
  quality management teams, 44
  team facilitator, 46
  team leader, 46
  team members, 46–47
  team recorder, 46
  team roles and responsibilities,
      45–46
  TQM panels, 44
  traditional management and
      integrated management
      compared, 47–48
  typical traditional management, 48
Organizer forms, 150–152
Outcome evaluation, 109

P

Paradigm, 146
Paradigm Shift, 146
Pareto charts, 38
Partnerships, 131
Performance, 146
Pie charts, 40
Policies, 146
Political/organisational development
    indicators, 111–112
Problem Solving, 146
  techniques form, 168
Process, 146
Process decision charts, 36

Process evaluation, 109
Process flow chart, 31–32
  symbols, 33–34
Process improvement teams form, 156
Procurement management, 15
Project Management, 1–2, 9–21
  activities, 13
  causes of project failures, 18–20
  closure, 12
  communication management, 15
  construction, 13
  cost management, 14
  design, 13
  execution, 12
  feasibility, 13
  human resources management, 15
  initiation, 11
  integration management, 14
  knowledge areas, 13–15
  life cycle, 11–12
  overview, 9–11
  performance metrics, 17–18
  planning, 11–12, 13
  principles, 12–13
  procurement management, 15
  projects, programs, and portfolio
      management compared,
      20–21
  projects and operations compared,
      17
  quality management, 14
  risk management, 15
  role and responsibilities of the
      project manager, 15–17
  scope management, 14
  time management, 14
  turnover and startup, 13
Project Planning and Management,
    xix, 115–119
  acceptance, 118
  analysis, 116
  definition, 116

design, 116
development, 116–117
implementation, 118
operational support, 119
preparation, 115
project close down, 119
review, 118
testing, 118
Project Proposal Template, 126–136
background and justification, 127
equipment, 136
Executive Summary, 126
glossary, 126
management arrangements and
reporting, 132
objectives, 128
participants (target groups) of the
project, 130
partnerships, 131
program activities, 131–132
program goals, 131
program objectives, 131
project design and proposal
development, 130
project implementation and
management, 133–134
project monitoring and evaluation,
134
project personnel, 134–135
project plan, 129
strategic approach, 131
subcontracts, 135
summary of the project, 128–129
sustainability and disengagement,
132
table of contents, 126
training, 135–136
Project Sustainability, xviii, 1, 3–9
adaptability, 6
analysis, 2
audit ability, 6–7
characteristics, 6–7

dimensions, 5
examples and principles, 5–6
extensibility, 7
implement ability, 7
maintainability, 7
manageability, 7
measurement, 8
scalability, 7
social sustainability performance
metrics, 9
Project Sustainability Management
(PSM), xviii, xix, 3, 146–147
change management, 27
checklist, 26–28
communication channels, 28
financial planning and analysis, 24
financing, 27
identification of stakeholders and
advocates, 24
implementation, 64
legislation, 27
monitoring and evaluation, 25
overview, 22–23
plan, 23–25
program adaptation to changes,
24–25
program mission, vision, philosophy,
and values, 24
program report documentation, 25
program summary, 23
project deliverables, 27
project periodic updates, 26
quality assurance, 28
results orientation, 24
risk management, 27
strategies, 27
structure, 25
support systems, 25
sustainability society indexes, 25–26
team selection, 27

Q

Quality, 147
  assurance, 67–68
  audit, 65
  benchmarks, 67
  control, 67
  documentation, 63
  in fact, 66–67
  improvement structure form, 155
  leadership, 89–90
  management, 14
  management teams, 44
  measurement, 67
  in perception, 67
  plan process, 120–121
  project organization, 121
  project policy, 121
  project processes, 121
  in strategic implementation plan, 61
Quality Assurance (QA), xix, 28, 147
Quality Audit, 65, 147
Quality Control (QC), xix, 147

R

Relationship diagrams, 36
Research, 147
Resource, 148
Risk management, 15, 27
  process, 122
Roles and responsibilities form, 157
Run charts, 39

S

Scatter diagrams, 41
Shewhart, Walter A., 84
Shingo, Shigeo, 85
Six Sigma Methodology, xix, 91–94
  methodologies, 92–94
S.M.A.R.T. technique (Specific,
  Measurable, Attainable, and
  Realistic, Timely), 2–3

Social development indicators, 110–111
Stanford Research Institute, 103
Strategic implementation plan (SIP),
  51–69
  assessment, 58
  awareness program, 61
  benefits, 68–69
  budget development, 61
  certification and registration, 66
  commitment by top management,
    53–54
  completion of the written plan, 59
  continuous quality improvement,
    66–68
  developing strategies, goals, and
    objectives, 58–59
  development of an organizational
    structure, 59–60
  development of corporate strategic
    plan, 54–59
  documentation, 63
  document control, 64
  implementation, 64
  individual management skills, 68
  initial status survey, 62–63
  internal quality audit, 65
  management review, 65
  mission and vision, 57–58
  organizational improvement, 69
  overview, 51–52
  pre-assessment audit, 65–66
  quality council, teams, and panels,
    61
  quality system documentation, 63
  strategic planning and long-range
    planning, 55–56
  strategic planning model, 56
  training team leaders and
    facilitators, 62
Strategic Management, 148
Strategic Management Organization
  (SMO) Culture, xix

Strategy, 148
Structure, process, and output, components, 169
Subcontracts, 135
Sustainability, 148
Sustainable development, concept, xvii–xx
Sustainable Implementation Plan (SIP), xix
Sustainable organizational structure, 42–50
Sustainable Process Development, 29–41
   process flow chart, 31–32
   process flow chart symbols, 33–34
   total quality management, 30–31
   tools, 34–37
Sustainable project management processes, 114–115
   administration, 115
   controlling, 115
   directing, 114
   planning, 114
SWOT Analysis (Strengths, Weaknesses, Opportunities, and Threats), xix, 2–3, 102–105
   examples of activities, 104–105
   major considerations, 103–104
   opportunities, 105
   strengths, 104
   threats, 105
   weaknesses, 104–105
Syndrome, 148
System, 148

T

Team charter, 161–162
Team leaders
   drafting a team charter, 161–162
   training, 62

Team project record form, 166
Technology, 148
Time management, 14
Total Quality Control (TQC), 73
   International Organization for Standardization (ISO) series standards, 94–96
Total Quality Management (TQM), 1–2, 30–31, 148
   basic tenets, 80–81
   commitment, 80–81
   continuous improvement, 80–81
   culture, 85–87
   differences between traditional management and, 50
   as a foundation in business, 87–88
   framework, 79
   fundamentals, 70–73
   history, 72, 88–89
   integrated management, 49–50
   panels, 44
   paradigm shift, 74
   principles, 72–73, 74–79
   procedural steps, 88
   quality leadership, 89–90
   statistical tools, 37–41
   tools, 34–37
Training, 136
   team leaders and facilitators, 62
Tree diagrams, 35

U

Unemployment Rate, 149
Utility, 149

V

Value Management, 149
Value Management Study, 149

W

Waitley, Dennis, 77
Weekly organizer, 151
William McDonough Architects, xviii
Work, 149
World Commission on Environment
        and Development, xvii

ABOUT THE AUTHOR

Mr. John N. Morfaw (alias Sir Johnny Mor) is a Project Management/ Sustainable Management Consultant by career and based in the Washington DC Metropolitan Area.

Mr. John Morfaw hails from the Republic of Cameroon, West Africa, where he earned a Diploma at the School of Social Studies (ENAAS) Yaounde, and another Diploma in Project Planning and Management from the Pan-African Institute for Development (PAID), Buea. He was awarded a scholarship as an Exchange Student to the USA through the Council of International Programs in Cleveland, Ohio in 1990. During the program he had orientation on American history, politics, social, cultural and academic policies at Cleveland State University. He also took classes as a Graduate Audit Student at the Mandel School of Applied Social Sciences, Case Western Reserve University, and Cleveland, Ohio. He later moved to Pennsylvania and obtained a Masters of Business Administration (MBA) Lincoln University of the Commonwealth of Pennsylvania in 1999. In 2005 he was earned a Graduate Certificate in Project Management from the Graduate School of Professional Studies at Penn State University-Great Valley, Malvern, Pennsylvania.

Mr. John Morfaw currently works as a Facilitator/Trainer with Rescare Workforce Empowerment Services of Prince George's County, Maryland, USA. He is the Founder and Chief Executive Officer (CEO) of Tanyimor Project Inc. and Tanyimor Foundation Inc. He is also the Coordinator of Strategic Management Services with the Institute for Research in Global Business (IRGB). Mr. Morfaw is a Community Advocate and Activist, involved in many other community activities with both national and internal organizations around the world. He is also a member of the Advisory Boards of The Sustainability Institute of Clarion University of Pennsylvania and a mentor with the Africa Unbound Mentorship Program. He has participated in various World Bank Africa Diaspora Program Network conferences and "Africa Plan of Action" consultative meetings towards the attainment of the Millennium Development Goals.

He is married to Pamela Asangong Morfaw (Lady Pammy MOR), a Certified Clinical Research Scientist with the National Institute of Health NIH) in Bethesda, Maryland, USA... They have two beautiful girls-Nkeng MOR and Muyang MOR, popularly known as the "The MOR Sisters".

Website: www.tanyimorproject.com;
Email: sirjohnmor@yahoo.com

MARKETING FLYER

This book provides an evaluative analysis of the relationship between a good strategic implementation plan and the efficiency and effectiveness in implementation in order to enhance the sustainability of a project in the marketplace. It elaborates on the various project sustainability metrics, characteristics, measurement, indexes and parameters involved in the effective and efficient implementation of projects. Various aspects of project sustainability such as financial, economic, social, cultural, political, legal, environmental and educational are explored for a comprehensive approach for project implementation. The book also provides an exhaustive elaboration on the theories of management postulated by the Gurus of Total Quality Management such as Edward Deming, Joseph Juran, Philip Crosby, Walter Shewhart, Kaoru Ishikawa and Shigeo Shingo. Other contemporary business concepts such as Six Sigma Methodology, International Organization for Standardization (ISO), Capacity Building, Knowledge Management, Configuration Management, and S.W.O.T Analysis, the S.M.A.R.T Techniques which help in project monitoring and evaluation and ultimate sustainability are discussed. The book elaborates on the Project Sustainability Management (PSM) concept which gives room for effective and efficient implementation of various sustainability processes, systems, structures and other activities. It also provides a series of Project Sustainability Management training forms and templates for various project management processes and a very comprehensive and elaborate Strategic and Sustainable Implementation Plan (SIP).

Mr. John N. Morfaw holds an MBA from Lincoln University of the Commonwealth of Pennsylvania and a Graduate Certificate in Project Management from Penn State University Graduate School of Professional Studies, Great Valley, Malvern, Pennsylvania. He is the Founder and Chief Executive Officer (CEO) of Tanyimor Project

Inc. and Tanyimor Foundation Inc. Mr. John Morfaw is an Advisory Board Member of the Sustainability Institute at Clarion University of Pennsylvania, and the Coordinator of the Strategic Management Program at the Institute for Research in Global Business (IRGB). He is a Mentor with the Africa Unbound Mentorship Program. Mr. Morfaw has participated in various World Bank Africa Diaspora Network conferences and "Africa Plan of Action" consultative meetings towards the attainment of the Millennium Development Goals.

Lightning Source UK Ltd.
Milton Keynes UK
UKOW021318181011

180505UK00001B/25/P